Can We Save the Common Market?

MAINSTREAM SERIES

Editors: Lord Blake, Leon Brittan, Jo Grimond,
John Patten and Alan Peacock

MALCOLM RUTHERFORD

Can We Save the Common Market?

Basil Blackwell · Oxford

First published 1981
Basil Blackwell Publisher Limited
108 Cowley Road
Oxford OX4 1JF
England

British Library Cataloguing in Publication Data

Rutherford, Malcolm
    Can we save the Common Market? (Mainstream series)
    1. European communities.
    I. Title   II. Series
    341.24'22   HC241.2
ISBN 0-631-12933-2

Typesetting by Freeman Graphic, Tonbridge
Printed in Great Britain by Billing and Sons Ltd.,
Guildford, London, Oxford, Worcester

CONTENTS

PREFACE

The title of this book — *Can We Save the Common Market?* — is not my own. When it was first suggested by my friends Leon Brittan and John Patten, it seemed to me both ambiguous and arrogant. Who are 'we'? Assuming that this means the British, surely the European Economic Community, the EEC, could get along well enough without us? There is also a narrower interpretation: can we save British membership? And if so, for what?

In journalism, titles that end with a question mark are taken to imply that the writer does not know the answer. One night at the *Financial Times* about 15 years ago, their use was categorically forbidden by the then editor when he found that almost every headline on the foreign news pages was followed by a query. The writ has remained in force to this day, though few people remember where it came from.

I am not sure that I know the answer to the title's question myself. In any case, it would be foolish to give it away before the final chapter. But I have certainly taken liberties with the question. I should like the 'we' in the title to extend to my friends and contemporaries in continental Europe, of whom I sometimes have more hopes than of those in Britain. What I have tried to do is to describe the different attitudes to the Community in different member countries and to find some areas where progress might be made.

Since I was asked to write the book, there has been one major development: the British government has secured an interim agreement to relieve its contribution to the Community budget. It now looks as if the whole Community will have to discuss its own future towards the end of this year, otherwise it will be in danger of running out of funds. Perhaps for the first time, Britain will take part in these negotiations as an equal partner rather than a recalcitrant member pleading a special case.

Yet there has been no perceptible change in British public opinion. If anything, it has continued to move steadily against British membership. The choices lie between taking the opportunity to reform the Community from within, protracting a relatively unhappy marriage, or declaring for divorce — with or without popular consent. I prefer the first.

CHAPTER 1

Opinion in Europe

In Europe the Common Market is popular and taken for granted. In Britain it seems to be neither of these. Within the old Six original members it would scarcely occur to anyone to conduct an opinion poll about staying or leaving. In Britain it happens all the time, with results that we shall explore further in the next chapter. The main question which divides opinion in continental Europe is whether integration is being pursued fast enough, and even there the divide is between those who regard the present pace as adequate and those who would rather go faster. Hardly anyone wants the pace to be slowed down; still less do they want the Community to be scrapped. According to the polls, greater integration is quite as strongly favoured in France, which is often considered the odd man out, as it is in West Germany, which used to be seen as a pace-setter.

The one exception in continental Europe is Denmark, which, like Britain and Ireland, joined the Community in 1973 in the first enlargement. The Danes regularly carry out opinion polls about the benefits of staying in, and the balance is only just in favour. Indeed, if the Community were to be reformed in the way that successive British governments have wanted, Danish membership would probably be in doubt. The Danes, already rich in terms of income per head, are net beneficiaries from the common

1

agricultural policy (CAP), which is precisely what the British want changed. British and Danish interests are in fundamental conflict.

The Irish are net beneficiaries all round, but at least have the excuse of being poor. Even one of the most formidable critics of the present financial workings of the Community, Mr Wynne Godley, the Director of the Department of Applied Economics at the University of Cambridge, has admitted that the one good aspect of the system is what it does for Ireland. The Irish are still by far the poorest Community member, but they receive the largest benefit per head. Not only has their prosperity increased as a result of membership; they have also gained in political confidence. The Irish government did not use to host summit meetings for European leaders at which the British Prime Minister played second or third fiddle to the President of France and the Chancellor of the Federal Republic. So it is not surprising that the Community should be popular in Ireland, though here again opinion could change if the EEC placed less emphasis on agriculture.

What concerns us now, however, is not so much the peripheries as the differences of opinion between Britain and the original Six. Since 1973, the year of enlargement, the Brussels Commission, using the most reputable outside agencies, has sponsored a series of polls on the development of opinion within the Community. The detailed results can be found in *Euro-baromètre,* usually published twice a year by the Commission.

For the British observer there are two really striking findings. The first is the way that British opinion differs from that of the Six, and the second is the way that French opinion − for all its reputation of being devious, Gaullist, nationalistic, obstreperous or whatever − is generally in line with that of the continental partners.

The question is repeatedly asked, for example, whether

the electorates of the individual states see Community membership as a good or a bad thing. In France the percentage regarding it as bad has never even touched ten, and even that figure is high in comparison with some other members. In Italy, the Netherlands, Belgium and Luxembourg, the percentage has only rarely touched five. Only in Germany was the 10 per cent mark ever breached, and that by a whisker. In Britain, as we shall see later, the figure has never fallen below 20 per cent, has usually risen above 30 per cent, and is now above 50 per cent. Among the old Six the numbers who regard membership of the Community as a bad thing are politically and statistically insignificant.

There is another more complex question posed on behalf of the Commission which goes as follows: 'Some people consider the Common Market as being a first step towards a closer union between the member states. Personally, do you yourself think the movement towards the unification of Europe should be speeded up, slowed down, or continued as it is at present?'

The question should be examined closely before coming to any judgement about the answers. The second sentence does not necessarily follow logically from the first. It would be possible to be in favour of faster progress towards the unification of Europe without in any way approving of the present organisation of the Common Market; such, presumably, is the position of some British pro-Marketeers. The phrase 'unification of Europe' is also undefined, which is possibly why it is used so often in the communiqués of European foreign ministers and heads of government. Finally, it is rather difficult to imagine that the majority at least of continental Europeans would be against the unification of Europe. One would hardly expect them to opt for its division.

These ambiguities perhaps explain why the British response to the question is not quite as hostile as might have been expected given what the other polls show about

British attitudes to the Community in general. Yet there is still a marked difference between British opinion and that of the old Six. Among the Six the percentage wanting slower progress towards the unification of Europe is negligible. It has been at its highest in France and Germany, but again usually well within single figures. In Italy the percentage has never risen about five and in 1979 was running at two. Among the Six as a whole the idea that progress towards unification should be deliberately delayed is obviously not taken seriously.

There is the touch of a division among the Six about the pace. The Italians are by far the most eager for acceleration, no doubt because of their domestic political problems. Italy, it seems to me, has never been quite confident as a nation state; it wants to be part of a wider union. Italian politics, though full of changes on the surface are essentially static. They do not reflect the vitality of Italian life. For the Italians, therefore, the development of Europe could be the answer. The figures have not changed all that much over the years, but in the poll at the end of 1979, 66 per cent of Italians said that they wanted faster progress. In France the figure was 35 per cent, and in Germany 43 per cent.

The differences seem much less significant, however, when you add together those who are satisfied with the present pace and those who want to accelerate. The average for the old Six on this score is 80 per cent, with 5 per cent wanting a slowdown and 15 per cent not replying. The figure for Germany is 80 per cent – spot on average – and for France 77 per cent. All these findings are from late 1979, but they are not vastly different from previous years. They hardly suggest much opposition among the Six to the idea of closer European union, and the supposedly deviant French seem to share broadly the same attitudes as their original partners.

The British figures are rather more puzzling. There is an

appreciable percentage, ranging over the years between about 15 and 25, which wants the pace to be slowed down. That is much higher than in the old Six, but not as high as might have been expected. Those wanting acceleration have varied between 17 and 28 per cent. It is hard to spot a trend here because of the fluctuations, but it would be impossible to argue convincingly on the basis of the figures that British support for the unification of Europe has been falling off. It is just not as high as it is elsewhere. Those satisfied with the existing rate of progress have been consistently in the 40–50 per cent range.

The gloss one would put on the British figures is modified by the ambiguities of the question asked, which is not specifically about the Common Market. Probably a majority of Britons are still in favour of something loosely described as the unification of Europe. The answers to other questions suggest, however, that they are not convinced that the Common Market as it is now organised is bringing it about, at least to their own satisfaction.

The real deviants are the Danes, whose percentage support for faster unification is barely in double figures and hardly ever has been since the moment of entry. The number of Danes wanting progress to be slowed down has usually been above 30 per cent, and that despite the advantages of the common agricultural policy. If the present CAP is undermined, Danish membership may no longer be secure. In the struggle for reform there may also be a battle between Britain and Denmark, and perhaps between Britain and Ireland. It will not in any case be a straightforward negotiation between Britain and the Six, even if the Six themselves were united in their approach.

CHAPTER 2

Opinion in Britain

The trend of British public opinion is increasingly hostile to continued membership of the European Community. Indeed it seems only too likely that unless a British government actively seeks to persuade the electorate of the benefits of staying in, the trend will become very hard to reverse. A successful government campaign would need to demonstrate the tangible rewards that belonging to the Community has brought to the country, and may or will bring in the future. At the time of writing, there is little sign either of the tangible rewards or of a sustained government effort at persuasion.

It was once assumed that the question of membership was finally resolved as a result of the referendum in 1975. A memorable quote from Mr Anthony Wedgwood Benn on the day that the results were declared went as follows:

> I have just been in receipt of a very big message from the British people. I read it loud and clear... By an overwhelming majority the British people have voted to stay in and I am sure that everybody would want to accept that. That has been the principle of all of us who advocated the referendum.

Mr Benn was the Labour minister who, though he had

once been in favour of membership, had subsequently
turned against and who did more than almost anyone else
to bring about the referendum. On the night of 6 June
1975 when all the votes were in he accepted what appeared
to be reality. Of the 68 areas into which the country was
divided for the purposes of the poll, only the Shetlands
and the Western Isles had voted against continued membership on the terms renegotiated by the government of the
then Mr Harold Wilson. The vote in favour of staying in
was 67.2 per cent. The vote against was 32.8 per cent. It is
true that there were some regional variations: the Scottish
vote was around 10 per cent less favourable to the idea of
continued membership than the English. But in general the
result could not be disputed by anyone who believed in
the democratic process.

The British people had voted and done so in some
strength. The turnout was 65 per cent – far higher than
some European diplomatic observers in London had
believed possible, and not far short of the turnout in
general elections. Looking both backwards and forwards
from 1975, however, it can be shown that the result was
less of a turning point than an aberration. The electorate
was not voting on whether or not to join the Community
but on whether to stay in or face the consequences of
withdrawal, which was a very different matter. During the
campaign all the great issues of defence and security in a
hostile world were raised in a way that must have per-
suaded the bulk of the voters that life outside Europe
would be pretty lonely.

If there were to be another referendum in the 1980s, it
is possible that the same factors would prevail, though
even that is doubtful, as I shall go on to suggest. For the
really striking point about the aftermath of the referendum in 1975 was how quickly opinion swung back against
membership. In June of that year the British people voted
by a majority of more than two to one in favour of staying

in. Yet by September 1976 a Gallup poll conducted on behalf of the Brussels Commission found that 37 per cent of the British electorate regarded membership as 'a bad thing', while only 33 per cent saw it as beneficial. This is a trend which by and large has continued ever since, to the point where a similar Gallup poll in April 1980 showed 49 per cent of the electorate regarding membership as bad and only 23 per cent believing it to be good.

It is not generally realised that this is not just a recent development — tied, for example, to rising dissatisfaction about the size of the British net contribution to the Community budget. In fact, a study of the opinion polls over the years shows that the idea of membership has very rarely been popular, either before or after joining. Opinion was on the whole in favour of the pro-Marketeers in the very early 1960s, when it was first rumoured that the Macmillan administration was thinking about applying. The Gallup organisation has produced a report on its findings on British attitudes to the Common Market 1957—74. In July 1960 it asked: 'If the British Government were to decide that Britain's interest would best be served by joining the European Common Market, would you approve or disapprove?' The response was 49 per cent approval, 13 per cent disapproval and 38 per cent 'don't knows'. The interesting figure was the 'don't knows', presumably reflecting the general ignorance of the subject at the time. As the issue was more widely discussed, the number of 'don't knows' duly began to fall. On the eve of the Macmillan application in early August 1961, the response to the same question by Gallup was: 44 per cent approval, 22 per cent disapproval and 34 per cent 'don't knows'.

While the entry negotiations progressed, Gallup was conducting polls on an almost weekly basis. Support for prospective membership reached a peak in late October 1962, when the figures in answer to the same question read: approvals 58 per cent, disapprovals 22 per cent, 'don't knows' 20 per cent. Less than three months later General de Gaulle, who had perhaps been reading the polls, delivered his veto. For a while, the pollsters stopped covering the subject of whether Britain wanted to join the Community, no doubt for the good reason that there was no point in asking utterly hypothetical questions. If there was no possibility of joining because of French opposition, the issue was dead.

Gallup came back into the field in 1965, when the Wilson government was toying with the idea of a renewed application. The findings, in answer to the old question, in February of that year were: approvals 59 per cent, disapprovals 19 per cent, 'don't knows' 22 per cent. In other words, there appeared to have been no falling off in the support for membership despite General de Gaulle. Indeed, according to Gallup, support continued to rise in the next year or so. In July 1966 no less than 71 per cent of those polled said that they would approve of entry. Only 12 per cent said that they would disapprove, and the 'don't knows' came down to 17 per cent.

According to the opinion polls at any rate, which are the best measure that we have, British support for membership had never been as high before; nor has it ever been as high again. After July 1966 sentiment in favour of joining, though it had its ups and downs, steadily fell away. The Wilson government had been re-elected with a more than working majority on 31 March 1966. It finally made the application for membership in May 1967. Just after it did so Gallup changed its question to: 'The Government has decided that Britain's interest would best be served by joining the Common Market and they have applied for membership. Do you approve or disapprove of their application to join?' The results were that only 35 per cent approved, while 44 per cent disapproved and 21 per cent said that they didn't know. It seems to have been the first time that there was at least a simple majority against belonging to the Community. It was by no means the last.

The Wilson application did not get very far. What is usually known as General de Gaulle's second veto occurred in November 1967. Afterwards sampling of public opinion on the membership question again tended to cease for a while. On 18 June 1970 the Conservatives rather surprisingly won the British general election under the leadership of Mr Edward Heath, perhaps the British European *par excellence*. There had been one very striking event in the meantime. In April 1969 General de Gaulle had resigned, to be succeeded as French President by the more flexible and pragmatic Georges Pompidou. The new negotiations on British accession to the Community began on 30 June 1970. Gallup by then was already back in action.

The results of those polls are revealing. At no stage during the Heath negotiations did support for the principle of applying for membership rise above 30 per cent. The highest degree of support registered by Gallup was in June 1971, when the negotiations were nearing completion following the successful meeting between Mr Heath and President Pompidou in Paris the previous month. In answer to the question: 'Do you approve or disapprove of the Government applying for membership of the European Common Market?', the Gallup finding read: approve 27 per cent, disapprove 58 per cent, don't know 15 per cent. A few months earlier, in November 1970, the level of approval had been down to 16 per cent and of disapproval up to 66 per cent.

Britain finally joined the Community in January 1973. On the eve of entry Gallup asked the question: 'On the facts as you know them, are you for or against Britain joining the Common Market?' The findings were: for 39 per cent, against 45 per cent, don't know 16 per cent. Those figures hardly convey an overwhelming popular endorsement almost on the day that membership became a reality.

After accession Gallup continued to poll, though the

question had been changed to: 'Do you think that we were right or wrong to join the Common Market?' In January 1973 the response was 38 per cent right, 36 per cent wrong, 26 per cent 'don't know'. There was a very slight rise in the percentage approving membership in the few following months, but the percentage of those disapproving rose even faster. The 'don't knows' were apparently moving against belonging to the Community. For example, in February 1974 — the month in which Mr Heath lost a general election — a Gallup poll suggested that only 28 per cent believed that Britain had been right to join. 58 per cent believed that the decision had been wrong and the 'don't knows' fell to 14 per cent.

From January 1973 Gallup introduced a second, more probing question. It went: 'If you were to be told tomorrow that the Common Market had been scrapped, would you be sorry about it, indifferent or pleased?' The question was repeated on an almost monthly basis until January 1975. The percentage saying that they would be sorry never touched 30 and at one stage (February 1974) fell below 20. The percentage saying that they would be pleased was never below 30, was usually in the 40s and several times came very close to 50. Those who replied 'indifferent' were in the 20–30 per cent range throughout. The 'don't knows' averaged around 10 per cent.

The most favourable pro-Market interpretation of those findings required assuming that, in the last resort, all those who claimed indifference to the Community's demise plus all those who declared ignorance would switch to the camp of those who said that they would be sorry. Even then, the resulting aggregate would at times have had only the barest of majorities. And of course the assumption of the wholesale switch would have been wildly unrealistic. At least some of those who professed themselves either indifferent or ignorant would have gone the other way.

On the basis of the opinion polls, therefore, at least

from 1967 onwards the anti-Marketeers had reasonable grounds for thinking that a referendum on British membership could lead to a vote for withdrawal. What they and the pollsters seem to have overlooked, however, was the question of saliency, or how strongly people felt about the matter. In other words, it was one thing to say that you were against membership when asked a hypothetical question in an opinion poll, but it did not necessarily mean that you thought the issue very important either way. Your response might simply have been registering your dissatisfaction with the government of the day on quite other matters. The Common Market indeed was probably as useful a scapegoat as any for prevailing discontents. It was another thing altogether to vote to get out when a referendum actually took place and practically the whole of the Establishment – in the widest sense of that word – was trying to persuade you to vote to stay in.

The Wilson government thus had an advantage in the referendum which years of opinion polls had not brought out. The government, or at least the bulk of it, had come to the conclusion that membership was right for Britain, but it wanted to renegotiate the terms and to hold a popular vote on the result with the aim of settling the argument, especially within the Labour Party, once and all. One of its great assets was that the great mass of the Conservative Party was ready to join the campaign for a 'yes' vote. That meant that perhaps 30–40 per cent of the electorage would be basically in favour of staying in for a start. But there was another more tactical asset. The government did at least go through the motions of renegotiation, and was seen to do so. (As a matter of fact it omitted to renegotiate one of the most troublesome issues of all and the one on which it had the best case, namely the common fisheries policy, because the Ministry of Agriculture never thought to mention it and the Foreign Office never thought to prompt it. Resolution of the fisheries policy remained outstanding several years later. But that is an historical footnote.)

When the Wilson administration had renegotiated the terms it was able to turn to the country and say words amounting to: 'Look, here's a better deal which we, or at least most of us, are prepared to recommend and, what is more, we are prepared to put it to the test of popular acceptance, which is more than the Conservatives ever did.' In retrospect, the renegotiation looks even more synthetic than it did at the time, though the political ploy of attempting to unite the Labour Party by putting the issue to the people did seem to work — for a while.

The point is made very clearly in the standard work on the subject, *The 1975 Referendum* (Macmillan, 1976), by David Butler and Uwe Kitzinger. At the very time when Gallup and other polls were finding a majority of the electorate, with varying degrees of emphasis, opposed to British membership, a private poll conducted on behalf of the government in August 1974 suggested that 76 per cent favoured a referendum. It was then found in a number of polls that the response about membership was quite different if the old familiar questions was rephrased to: 'If the Government renegotiated new terms for Britain's membership of the Common Market and they thought it was in Britain's interests to remain a member, how would you vote then — to stay in or leave it?' As early as August 1974 the response to that question among voters who claimed to have made up their minds was 69 per cent in favour of staying in and 31 per cent in favour of getting out. That was nine months before the referendum took place, and well before anything like a sustained campaign was under way. Oddly enough, it came remarkably close to the final result.

Several conclusions can be drawn from the way the vote went. The most obvious is the one that was drawn at the time by Mr Benn along with practically everyone else:

namely that the argument was over. The British people had voted by an overwhelming majority to stay in. Another is that the popular grouses against membership of the Community do not really run very deep. If and when the government of the day gives a clear lead in favour of belonging to the Community, the bulk of the electorate will be prepared to accept the advice and vote accordingly. For instance, if membership means a rise in the price of butter, the voters will put up with it if the promised reward is an increase in security.

Even at the time, however, more ambiguous readings of the referendum result were possible. The yes vote was achieved by the government pulling out all possible stops, being overwhelmingly supported by the Conservative opposition as well as by almost all the media, and by stressing the widest possible issues. The question of whether the majority of the British people actually liked the Common Market remained, and the evidence of the polls over the years was that they did not. Equally the question remained for the government – and its successors – of how to make the Community more popular.

In the run-up to the referendum the opinion polling became more sophisticated. Questions started to be put about the benefits or non-benefits of membership in specific areas. Respondents were asked for a judgement not only on such down-to-earth issues as the effect of membership on food prices, but also on more intangible issues such as Britain's role or bargaining power in the world. In general they thought that the effect on prices was harmful, but that it was a price worth paying for the sake of the broader benefits.

Looking back, people's discontent on the down-to-earth issues – which do after all affect them day in and day out – ought to have been taken more seriously at the time. It signalled that while the majority of the electorate might be ready to go along with the government on more strategic issues, the more practical benefits of membership were less than self-evident. There may also have been the hint of a signal that if some leading politicians more widely admired than Mr Benn or Mr Enoch Powell had embraced the anti-membership cause, and if some of the media had followed, the size of the 'yes' vote might have been less convincing. Mr Powell is a partial exception, but the evidence of the polls is that the politicians who were regarded as the most popular in the country were also those who advocated staying in. That must have had some effect.

It is clear now that neither the renegotiation nor the referendum changed anything fundamental about Britain's relationship with the Community. A political embarrassment for the Labour government was temporarily removed, but that was all. The mechanism designed to restrain the British contribution to the Community budget turned out to be defective. One of the factors on which financial redress depended was that Britain should be in substantial balance of payments deficit. Shortly afterwards the balance of payments moved into surplus, not least because of North Sea Oil. Thus, despite the renegotiation, Britain was still liable to pay an ever larger net contribution to the Community budget.

Again, the common fisheries policy had not been mentioned and the common agricultural policy had not been reformed. Moreover, once the referendum was out of the way the government did not conspicuously change its attitude to the Community. It continued to behave as a reluctant participant and was not above making the Community the scapegoat for domestic ills. In those circumstances it is not surprising that familiar British feelings about membership began to reassert themselves.

As already noted, the first post-referendum poll to find that public opinion was again turning against membership took place as early as September 1976. There were one or two fluctuations thereafter, but from mid-1978 onwards the general trend was increasingly hostile towards the Community. The latest Gallup poll conducted on behalf of the Brussels Commission at the time of writing was in April 1980. It suggested that only 23 per cent of the electorate regarded membership as 'a good thing', while 49 per cent thought it was bad. The previous poll, in October 1979, had shown figures of 29 and 41 per cent respectively. There is evidence that there may also have been a qualitative change in the sense that feelings now run much deeper. The Community may have ceased to be a minor irritant and become a major grievance, scarcely even to be given the benefit of the doubt on the so-called intangible rewards of membership.

A Gallup poll conducted for the *Sunday Telegraph* in April 1980 had the great merits not only of asking a series of detailed questions but also of being able to compare the findings with those at the time of the referendum. As one would expect, opinion was heavily against membership on all the basic day-to-day issues, though even here the change since 1975 was striking. For example, to a question about the price of food, 68 per cent of those polled said that Britain would be better out of the Community; only 12 per cent said that it would be better to stay in. The response to the same question at the time of the referendum had been that 34 per cent thought that Britain would be better off outside and 32 per cent inside. There followed a range of questions about non-food prices, the levels of wages and taxation, unemployment and the general standard of living. On all those matters more people said that Britain would be better placed outside the Community than in, often by a substantial majority. Just before the referendum, the response to exactly the same questions had been that it would be better to remain inside.

The response to the more abstract questions pointed to a change of opinion of a different kind. It appeared still to be accepted that membership has its advantages in terms of defence and foreign policy, but it was beginning to be a close-run thing. Asked about 'Britain's position in the world', an admittedly vague question but one to which politicians tend to attach some importance, 33 per cent of those polled thought that the country was better off inside the EEC, but 31 per cent thought the opposite. The ratio at the time of the referendum was 52 : 20. There was a rather stronger preference for staying in response to a question concerning 'Britain's voice in international affairs', but it was still only 34 per cent to 26 per cent. Five years before, the breakdown had been 48 to 18 per cent. The most positive response of all, though it was still far from overwhelming, concerned defence: 39 per cent of those polled thought that membership contributed to the defence of Britain, and 23 per cent thought that even on this question the country would be better off outside the Community. The ratio in 1975 was 49 : 14. From figures like those it is difficult to avoid the conclusion that even the old foreign policy reasons for membership no longer seem as convincing to the British public as once they did.

The same Gallup poll then went on to ask one or two general questions. For instance: 'Do you think that the British economy would be stronger in the Common Market or stronger out of the Common Market?' 56 per cent thought that it would be stronger outside; 22 per cent inside. The response at the time of the referendum had been 51 per cent inside, 25 per cent outside. Finally Gallup posed the question: 'If you could vote on whether we stayed in the Common Market or left it, how would you vote?' Only 27 per cent said that they would vote to stay in. 59 per cent said that they would vote to leave, while not the least interesting finding was that the 'wouldn't votes' and 'don't knows' were down to 7 per cent apiece. Such findings are not easy to reconcile with the view that British feelings about the Community do not run deep.

It may be argued that any findings of opinion polls

about Britain and Europe in April 1980 must have been atypical because of the special circumstances of the time. The size of the British net contribution to the Community budget had become a serious political issue, much more so than any concrete problem between Britain and Europe at the time of the Labour government's insistence on renegotiation of the terms of entry. Mrs Margaret Thatcher, the Conservative Prime Minister, was playing it for all it was worth, with the enthusiastic support of both sides of the House of Commons. She had already rejected Community offers of a settlement and appeared to have grown more popular at home for having done so. It was natural that public opinion should be aroused.

These would be fair reservations if only the polls had changed afterwards. For the British government did succeed in reaching an interim settlement of the budgetary question at the end of May 1980, and on terms more favourable than the great majority of observers had predicted; yet the Gallup poll in late June suggested if anything a hardening of opinion against the Community. 54 per cent of those polled said that they regarded membership as 'a bad thing' and only 22 per cent thought that it was good. In the previous month the ratio was 52 : 26, an insignificant variation perhaps when one allows for the usual margin of error, but certainly no encouragement from the pro-Marketeer's point of view.

A relatively new question by Gallup went as follows: 'Do you think the Government's policy on the Common Market has been too tough, not tough enough or about right?' Only 6 per cent thought that it had been too tough, 36 per cent thought that it had been about right, and 49 per cent thought that it had not been tough enough. That hardly read like an immediate vote of support for the budget compromise.

It is true that the government has not done much to defend the budget agreement, let alone to sell it. But that is part of the problem. If the government is not prepared to defend its own work and speak up for membership of the Community, how is it possible to reverse the tide of public opinion? In a way the situation after the interim budget settlement was reminiscent of the period following the referendum. The government had made some progress in its relationship with the Community, but there was little or no follow-up in the form of any attempt to explain the potential tangible benefits of membership.

There were other more adverse factors from the point of view of those who still believed in the Community. In the mid-1970s the dissatisfaction with Europe had come largely from the Labour Party; the Conservatives indeed had come to the aid of the Labour pro-Marketeers in the referendum campaign. By 1980, however, there could be little doubt that the Conservatives too were deeply divided, not so much in the Cabinet, nor even in the House of Commons, but in the country. The extent of the anti-Market sentiment as shown by the opinion polls could be explained in no other way, and it was the same message that Tory MPs brought back from their constituencies. The MPs may not have been in favour of withdrawal or anything like it, but they were not averse to beating the anti-Europe drum, especially when it concerned the French.

The most significant new factor of all was probably Mrs Thatcher herself. The Prime Minister had never been closely identified with the European cause and had played little part in the debates of the previous two decades. She was pro-Europe when she could relate it to defence, with which the Community has little if anything to do, but that was about all. She had fought publicly for an even better budget solution than the government finally accepted under the influence of Lord Carrington, the Foreign Secretary, and she did not go out of her way to welcome it. Above all, she must have been aware that popular feeling about the Community accorded with her own personal

instinct. She did not appear to be someone who would lightly abandon this link with popular sentiment for the sake of closer ties with Europe, and without her support it was very difficult for ministers to make speeches spelling out the Europe that might be.

None of this chapter should be taken as suggesting that British withdrawal from the Community is inevitable. For one thing it is very hard to imagine how the mechanics of withdrawal could operate. For another it still seems to me quite likely that if withdrawal were raised as a practical possibility, Britain would choose to stay in. It would be an exceedingly lonely world outside. But a study of the opinion polls over the years does show a steady and deepening erosion of support. This can only be repaired if British governments are prepared actively to defend the Community and if the Community offers Britain practical benefits. The alternative is to continue the long war of attrition that has been characteristic of British membership so far, though with little benefit either to Britain or to the Community.

Finally, it might be objected that this argument has relied too heavily on the evidence of opinion polls. Yet what else is there except one's own and other people's observations? Of course the polls can be wrong from time to time. There is the question of margin of error: a 33 per cent positive response and a 31 per cent negative means only that opinion is evenly divided. Even more, there is the question of saliency. Measured over the years, however, the trend seems unmistakable. The popular reaction also seems both intelligible and intelligent. Take this response to a question posed by Gallup about which Common Market member has the most influence. In April 1980, 43 per cent said France and 36 per cent said Germany. The question was then asked, who would have the most influence in five years' time. The response was 42 per cent Germany and 23 per cent France. One can argue about the percentages, but the general trend would not be out of line with expert predictions. The polls suggest that the British people remain to be convinced that membership of the European Community is part of their natural way of life. If anything, their instinctive beliefs have been growing stronger.

CHAPTER 3

New Opportunity or Last Chance?

In the early hours of 30 May 1980 the foreign ministers of the Nine, meeting in Brussels, finally reached agreement on the question that had provoked the biggest Common Market crisis since its enlargement in 1973: namely, the size of the British net contribution to the Community budget. The agreement was a surprise both for the fact that it was achieved at all and for its relative generosity towards Britain. Only a day or two before, senior Cabinet ministers in London,. including some of the most favourably disposed towards the Community, had been saying that the outlook was grim. Their opinion was shared by European diplomats. In the end it seems to have been the Italian chairmanship that won the day: Signor Emilio Colombo, the President of the Council, kept the foreign ministers at it until agreement was reached.

As Signor Colombo remarked somewhat sadly afterwards, in an interview with the Italian newspaper *La Repubblica*: 'Everybody has recognised that our Presidency has been active and profitable. May I add that this has been acknowledged more readily abroad than in Italy?' Certainly his efforts were appreciated by his fellow foreign ministers, and not least by the British Foreign Office.

22

It is significant that the agreement was achieved at the foreign minister level. Earlier efforts to settle the matter by heads of government — the so-called European Council — had led to some notably acerbic exchanges, with Mrs Thatcher demanding the return of 'her money' and pursuing a concept that Britain should not pay into the Community a penny more than it got back. The approach could scarcely be described as *'communautaire'*. President Giscard d'Estaing of France, who had originally devised the idea of the European Council as a means of allowing heads of state or government to have intimate chats about the future of Europe and the world, had objected that their sessions were now being asked to deal with questions that ought to have been settled lower down the hierarchy.

So the problem was resolved by foreign ministers *ad referendum,* which meant that it had to be referred back to national governments for final approval. Mrs Thatcher's approval was only reluctant. She saw that she had lost the card of being seen at home and in the House of Commons as standing up to the European Community, and she declined to recognise that the settlement was much better than almost all observers had predicted and considerably better than even the hopes of the Labour Party when in office. She had raised even higher expectations, and did not take easily to acceptance of reality. Mrs Thatcher played very little part in welcoming the Brussels agreement. It was, in short, more than expected but less than she wanted.

It was left to Sir Ian Gilmour, the deputy Foreign Secretary and a man who writes better than he speaks, to outline the settlement to the House of Commons on 2 June. Sir Ian claimed that the agreement was the 'culmination of a long and complex negotiation' which had begun shortly after the Conservative government took office in May 1979; in fact, the negotiation had been going on under Labour. But he put his finger on the main point when he said:

In the long term, the most important part of the package is the commitment of the Council to review the development of Community policies and the operation of the budget. . . . This review offers an opportunity that has never been available before, since we joined the Community, to work together with our partners for financial arrangements and Community policies that are to the advantage and interest of all the member states, as befits a Community of equals.

Sir Ian was right, but so in a way were Mrs Thatcher, with her reluctance to accept anything less than the whole loaf, and the growing band of critics who thought that Britain was unlikely ever to come to satisfactory terms with the Community. How could this be so? The fact is that the Brussels agreement was essentially temporary. As a permanent solution to the question of the British financial contribution, it was quite unacceptable. Its merit was that it bought time for further, more crucial negotiations towards substantially reshaping the Community's finances. The question was how this time would be used.

The budgetary crisis arose because Britain, the third poorest member of the Community after Ireland and Italy, was about to become its largest net contributor. It is possible to quibble about the precise figures, but not about their meaning. Perhaps the most generous way for a British writer to put it is to quote a French authority. M Jean François-Poncet, the French Foreign Minister, told the National Assembly on 4 June 1980, just after the Brussels agreement had been reached: 'Great Britain is in seventh place in the income scale per head of population. Its income stands at 80 per cent of the Community average. It stands at 133 per cent for the German Federal Republic and at 116 per cent for France.'

M François-Poncet went on:

> It is a fact, on the other hand, that Great Britain's net
> contribution to the Community budget was 850
> million units of account in 1979 and that it was to
> reach 1.8 billion units of account in 1980, rising to
> 2.5 billion units of account in 1981. As a comparison,
> the German Federal Republic, which is besides Great
> Britain the only other net contributor, paid into the
> Community budget 1.1 billion units of account in
> 1979 and this contribution will reach 1.2 billion units
> of account in 1980.

Mrs Thatcher could hardly have put it better, except perhaps in sterling. (The conversion rate at the time was 1.65
units of account to the pound.) There was an inequity
which plainly could not be allowed to continue.

As Sir Ian Gilmour told the House of Commons, the
Brussels agreement put a ceiling on the British net contribution in 1980 of £370 million. Since the contribution
had been expected to rise to £1.08 billion, the result was a
saving for the British Exchequer of over £700 million. For
1981, when the net contribution had been expected to rise
to £1.3 billion, there was to be a ceiling of £440 million.
All told that meant a saving on expected British expenditure of £1.57 billion. There were one or two other safety
mechanisms, plus a fallback formula designed to protect
Britain in 1982 should Community finances remain un-
reformed. But the details are not essential to the argument.
Britain had achieved a very substantial rebate. To put it in
perspective, Treasury ministers were then speaking of the
need to cut the public sector borrowing requirement by
£1 billion. They had been given £1.5 billion over two
years.

There was another way of looking at it, however. The
government had won a battle, but was not yet in a very

satisfactory position. Britain had ceased to be the largest net contributor to the Community budget only to become the second largest. It remained the third poorest member. As a result of the Brussels agreement, France moved from being more or less in balance with the Community to becoming a net contributor, but the British net contribution in 1980 and 1981 was going to be twice as large as the French. It was thus an interim solution and no more.

For the future, it was paragraph seven of the Brussels agreement that really mattered. This was the one that Sir Ian Gilmour had described in the House of Commons as providing the 'commitment of the Council to review the development of Community policies and the operation of the budget'. The paragraph reads:

> For 1982 the Community is pledged to resolve the problem by means of structural changes. The examination should concern the development of Community policies, without calling into question the common financial responsibility for these policies, which are financed from the Community's own resources, or the basic principles of the common agricultural policy. Taking account of the situations and interests of all member states, this examination will aim to prevent the recurrence of unacceptable situations for any of them. If this is not achieved, the Commission will make proposals along the lines of the 1980–81 solution and the Council will act accordingly.

The Commission was charged to produce its proposals for structural changes by the end of June 1981. (Structural changes was the jargon for saying that too much of Community expenditure went on agriculture, and that too much of that went on disposing of surpluses.) Agriculture indeed accounted for nearly 80 per cent of Community spending in 1979, and storing and then selling off the surpluses at subsidised prices accounted for nearly 80 per cent of that. The restructured budget would have to channel more resources to non-agricultural requirements. Sir Ian Gilmour was quite right in stating that this was the first time that Britain had been fully involved in a major reform of Community finance from the ground floor. The government was as free as that of any other member state to press its own proposals and to seek to reshape the Community from within. For this was no longer yet another British renegotiation; it was the Community as a whole looking to its future.

The significance of this point can hardly be understated. The main reason why Britain had become such a heavy net contributor in the first place was that the Community was weighted in favour of agricultural spending and agricultural rebates. If Britain had been in at the beginning, it could have resisted this tendency from the start. Its interests as a country with less than 3 per cent of the population on the land are fundamentally different from member-states where the farming community is up to 15 per cent. It is the built-in bias towards helping agriculture — almost at the expense of everything else — which the Community is now committed to review and revise.

There were several other reasons why the Brussels agreement was more important than it looked at first sight. Most of them lay in its timing. Neither heads of government nor foreign ministers could say so directly, but it was impractical to think of activating substantial reforms in 1980. The German elections were due in that year and took place in October. The French presidential elections took place in May 1981. Before the elections, for example, it was very difficult for Chancellor Schmidt of West Germany to advocate anything very much in the way of reform of the CAP for fear of alienating his junior coalition partner, the Free Democrats, which had a heavy dependence on the Bavarian farmers' vote. Equally, President Giscard was constrained by his own wish to be re-elected and the need not to alienate the Gaullists or the French farmers.

In the event, Giscard failed. The French elections produced a convincing victory for M François Mitterrand and were quickly followed by his Socialist Party winning an overall majority in the National Assembly. Some of his appointments were decidedly reassuring from the point of view of the European Community: for example, that of M Claude Cheysson, a former Brussels Commissioner, as Foreign Minister. M Cheysson also claimed to be something of an Anglophile.

With the French elections out of the way, there seemed the prospect of a clear run in which none of the major members of the Community would be inhibited in their European policies by short-term electoral considerations. There was, and there remains, the promise of much greater freedom of action.

After the Brussels agreement other problems were also known to be coming to a head. Greece entered the Community on 1 January 1981 as the beginning of the second enlargement. But Greece is a small country and can probably be coped with as one more poor member, rather like Ireland, in which both France and West Germany seem to take some kind of benign paternalistic interest. The real problem impending here was Spain and Portugal, whose entry had been envisaged for around 1983. Could the Community easily absorb a country as large as Spain, plus another as poor as Portugal? What would Spanish and Portuguese accession do to the EEC's financial system? Would it any longer be possible even to speak of the aim of economic convergence when the income level of the member countries was so obviously different?

Above all perhaps the Community of the Nine is already close to the limits of its agreed funding. Under the so-called 'own resources' system this is composed of:

the duties levied on imports entering the Community from third countries under the common external tariff;
levies charged on agricultural products from outside the Community to bring up their prices to the fixed levels prevailing under the CAP price support regime; and the yield of a notional value-added tax rate of up to 1 per cent.

It is likely that even the full 1 per cent yield from VAT, plus the other revenues, will be inadequate to meet Community expenditure by some time around the end of 1981. Something, therefore, will have to give. There will have to be less growth in expenditure, or more revenue, or a restructuring of the existing system. The three alternatives are not, of course, mutually incompatible.

It is clear now that although the Brussels agreement came about because of British opposition to insistence that the country was being unfairly treated, there were other factors at work. The continental Europeans were generally aware that the issue of the EEC's financial resources was approaching a turning point. There had at the very least to be a stock-taking which would raise such questions as: how much money should the Community spend, and on what? And how should the spending be financed in the interests of equity among the member states? The stock-taking was postponed until at least the second half of 1981, but it meant that there was a distinct possibility of change.

What was odd in the summer of 1980 was how much more readily — and certainly how much more obviously — this point was appreciated on the continent than in Britain. In London the general reaction to the Brussels agreement was one of relief that a crisis had been at least temporarily averted. The Community went out of the headlines, except in so far as the whole issue of membership continued to divide the Labour Party. In France the reaction was quite different and, one might say, much more realistic.

The French government was under no illusions about what had been conceded in Brussels, though to its credit it had been prepared to become a net contributor for the sake of reaching an accord. In June 1980 M Raymond Barre, the Prime Minister, and M Jean François-Poncet, the Foreign Minister, made a series of speeches and statements outlining their thoughts about what had happened and what should happen in future. Reporting to the National Assembly on 4 June, in a statement already partially quoted earlier in this chapter, M François-Poncet admitted that the examination of the British budgetary demands had 'underlined the excessive nature of some deficits' in the Community's finances. Perhaps it was the fact that France henceforth was going to have to help finance the deficits that brought about this change of view, but anyway here were the French admitting that not all was for the best in the workings of the common agricultural policy. The Foreign Minister then fully endorsed the idea of a complete review of the financial rules of the Community by June 1981. The real negotiations between member states would start after that.

Winding up the Assembly debate that followed, M Barre went further. Indeed he gave a remarkably frank account of the differing French and British approaches to the Community over the years, and indicated that he had in no way been surprised by the British behaviour; if anything he had expected the British to be much tougher, much earlier. The French, he said, had always had reservations about the original enlargement because it was likely to change the nature of the Community. This should not be interpreted as a sign of French hostility to Britain, but was merely a statement of fact.

M Barre continued:

We know perfectly well, looking at things as they really are, that we have a common agricultural policy which was designed for producer countries, for countries with a farming population, for countries capable of self-sufficiency which for the sake of an agriculture that they wish to keep active and expand are ready to put up with certain sacrifices, while the country entering the Community was one that had long since given up major agricultural activity, was an importing country and tied for very many reasons to countries outside the Community and outside Europe.

The difference between the French concept of a Community designed to protect agriculture and the British hankering after a free trade area in industrial goods could hardly have been put more clearly.

In a moment of self-justification, M Barre added:

We thought in 1969, that is the French government of the time thought in 1969, that the historical, economic and structural reasons were no longer so decisive. For those who witnessed the negotiations, and for myself in particular, I must tell you that what is happening seems to be to be occurring a little late compared with what could be foreseen.

But there could be no doubt about his conclusion. The French would fight to the utmost to preserve their own interests in the agricultural policy – and especially Community preference – yet fundamental change was taking place. The Prime Minister ended:

What I would also like to say to you is that the government is well aware that developments in the operation of the common agricultural policy call for

measures, for revisions, not a revision of the prin-
ciples — and I stress this — but of the manner in
which this policy is operated. It will be necessary,
since in the months and years ahead similar problems
will crop up again, for the French thinking in particular of the Federal Republic of Germany — to think
about improving the manner in which the common
agricultural policy is operated.

There was no mention of Britain in the peroration. It was
to Germany that France would turn. But still the message
was unmistakable. France had accepted that the common
agricultural policy was not functioning as well as it might,
and that financial constraints would impose reform.

Both M Barre and M François-Poncet were to return to
the subject in the next few weeks. It had certainly hit
them, even if it had not fully hit the British, that the
Brussels agreement radically called in question the future
organisation of the Community. They saw the connection
between putting a limit on the net budgetary contributions
of individual member states, the costs of further enlargement and the fact that the Community was approaching its
agreed budgetary ceiling. Thus M François-Poncet admitted in the National Assembly on 11 June 1980 that it was
more than likely that Britain would want permanently to
reduce its net contribution to the budget, and not just for
the period covered by the Brussels agreement. In that case,
the Foreign Minister went on, the Community would be
even more obliged to examine lasting adjustments to the
financial rules. There would then have to be a 'levelling off
of deficits and surpluses' — a clear reference to the mal-
functioning of the CAP. As long as the new financial rules
had not been defined, he added, it would be extremely
difficult satisfactorily to conclude negotiations with Spain
and Portugal.

There was also the question of the existing ceiling on

EEC spending: 'We are slowly reaching this ceiling and the additional exemptions necessitated by the reduction granted to Great Britain have brought us closer to this deadline.'

M François-Poncet then posed a series of questions, awareness of which had already been causing diplomatic and political flutters in Madrid and Lisbon:

If Spain and Portugal, who are placed ninth and twelfth in the Community in regard to gross national product per head of population, enter the Common Market, it is clear that these states will not be 'contributors' but beneficiaries. Where will the money come from? From new resources yet to be defined? Will it come from savings in expenditure? In this case, which section of the budget will they affect? Frankly, how can one conclude negotiations without being able to give clear answers on these points to those who wish to become members of the Community?

Of course, a good deal of that statement could have been for political and diplomatic effect. The Minister was showing his awareness of the wider issues, and looking for bargaining counters. Was it, for example, Britain who wanted to risk blocking the entry of Spain and Portugal by insisting on a limit on its own budgetary contribution? Or should the 1 per cent VAT limit perhaps be exceeded? One should not insult the French by believing that they never have ulterior motives. Still, the general thrust of the François-Poncet statement was right: there is bound to be a link between determining the net contributions of the Nine, enlargement of the EEC, and keeping or changing the 1 per cent ceiling.

M Barre returned to the subject when he made a speech — described by official French sources as of fundamental importance — to the German chambers of commerce and industry in Trier on 20 June. Again he was quite explicit about the origins of the Community and the French interests in it. France, he said, had entered the Community as much for political as for economic reasons. He went on:

> The construction on our continent of an organised economic area seemed to France to be dictated by the evolution of the world economy. At the same time, she saw it as a decisive contribution to a political organisation of Western Europe, based on a permanent reconciliation between France and Germany and close cooperation between these two countries. . . .
>
> To achieve these fundamental objectives France accepted in 1958 the free movement of industrial products, with all the disadvantages this involved at the time for her economy. She did so on condition that there would be a genuine common market for agricultural products to complement it. This 'contract' is the Community's true foundation.

It was left slightly unclear whether the 'contract' referred to was between agriculture and industry in particular or between France and Germany in general. But the drift was plain: France was again appealing to Germany. 'The Rome Treaty,' M Barre repeated, 'was designed for a Community of six.' It reflected their 'interests, aspirations and habits', and not those of the United Kingdom.

The French Prime Minister then went on to describe the British attitude to the Community as he saw it. Whatever his motives, he came very close to the truth:

> The British government, feeling that the time was drawing near when it would cease being outside a continental organisation which it viewed with apprehension, aware too of all that participation in the Community could bring Great Britain, abandoned its traditional caution and contracted commitments

which it hoped that, in time, it would become economically able to honour and its reluctant citizens able to accept. Unfortunately, you cannot keep on for a long time pretending that things are not as they really are.

That statement, with its stress on the reluctant citizenry and the very term 'a continental organisation', might almost have come from Mr Enoch Powell, the arch British opponent of membership. So might that last remark: 'You cannot keep on for a long time pretending that things are not as they really are.' There was a difference, however, between these two logicians. The French Prime Minister was accepting that Britain — the old Trojan horse — was inside the Community and, as a result of the Brussels agreement and what led up to it, had the power to try to change it. Mr Powell's hope lay in the possibility that the opportunity would not be used.

In the same Trier speech M Barre underlined the connection between reorganising the Community's financial arrangements and enlargement to include Spain and Portugal:

Common sense forces us to recognise that it is not possible to negotiate seriously with Spain and Portugal so long as we are not clear about what we can really negotiate, so long as we do not know what adjustments we are going to have to make to the Community's budgetary mechanisms and have not decided on how we can finance the tasks we shall have to take on owing to its southward enlargement. Clearly, the Community is at a turning point.

M François-Poncet made the point even more bluntly in a speech to the French Senate on 27 June: 'For the accession negotiations to make headway, there must be *prior settlement* [my italics] of the Community's internal problems, particularly those that have just been brought to light by Great Britain's requests.'

If there were any remaining doubts about how seriously the French were considering the future of the Community, and the need to safeguard their own position in it, M Barre sought to dispel them in a speech, in the presence of Mrs Thatcher, to the Franco-British Council in Bordeaux on 19 September 1980. The French Prime Minister in effect summarised what he had said in Trier about France having accepted sacrifices for the sake of the construction of Europe. For example: 'I shall merely remind those who today make much of the farming advantages France has gained from the Common Market of the efforts our industry and our entire country have made to break with a powerful protectionism and accept competition.' Then he turned directly to the common agricultural policy:

> We are, of course, wholly prepared to study improvements to it, but we shall remain adamant as to the basic principles: market and price unity, financial solidarity, Community preference. I hear it said here and there that this policy is absurd. I tend to answer with Lord Balfour's wisdom: 'It is better to do an absurd thing which has always been done than a wise thing which has never been done.'

The reference to Balfour smelled slightly as if someone had been burning the midnight oil over the Dictionary of Quotations, and the sentiment reduces conservatism to the point of sterility. But M Barre went on:

> Yet is it so absurd of the Community countries to want to safeguard the resources provided by their agriculture and which ensure security of supplies for their populations, when they suffer cruelly from the lack in their soil and subsoil of other resources, a fact

of which the latter's producers take advantage, if necessary by abusing the economic power conferred by a monopoly situation?

The last part of that sentence is obscure. It could be taken as an invitation – or a challenge – to the British to pool their energy resources within the European Community. It might equally well have been a challenge or invitation to the Organisation of Petroleum Exporting Countries (OPEC). To a British audience, however, the message should have been unmistakable. It was the culmination of so many French speeches over the summer – ever since the Brussels agreement. The French realised that the future of the Community was all to play for, and they were determined to have their say in shaping its development. The very frequency of the speeches, and the level from which they were made, indicated that initially at least they took the problem – and the possibilities – more seriously than the British. It was not until November that senior British ministers began to make their own speeches about how the Community might be reformed, and then only in one sudden burst.

The German reaction to the Brussels agreement was more muted, partly no doubt because the country was in the middle of an election campaign in which the governing coalition went increasingly on the defensive about the role of public expenditure in general. The opposition parties argued that state debt had been rising to dangerous levels, and while the government could not admit this in public, there was evidence behind the scenes that it was distinctly disturbed. The independent Bundesbank (central bank) gave its own warning about the level of government spending in its monthly report for September 1980, and there was a general expectation that, once the election was out of the way, the new government would go in for financial retrenchment.

The German economy was also in a transitional phase. It no longer had the familiar landmarks of a strong and appreciating currency and a balance of payments surplus. Even the balance of trade went into deficit in August and there were forecasts from the Bundesbank, since broadly fulfilled, of a current account deficit of some DM 30 billion for the year as a whole. The rise in oil prices and perhaps slipping German competitiveness in other ways had taken their toll. Graf Lambsdorff, the Economics Minister, caused a political storm in the summer when he suggested that Germans no longer worked hard enough. He may have exaggerated, but certainly there were signs that the Japanese were beginning to penetrate (say) the German car market in a way that they had never attempted before. The Bundesbank was actually warning of severe import pressures. There may have been no great cause for alarm, but at least temporarily the German economy was stumbling. In early 1981 the D-mark was subject to intense downward pressures.

The need to contain expenditure at home naturally had its effect on attitudes towards spending in Europe, not least because the Germans believed that they had already undertaken a wider international role on such matters as Western aid to Turkey. The government in Bonn saw that as its contribution to an international division of labour, or burden-sharing, but it was not prepared to keep on picking up the tab indefinitely. Thus it began to take a noticeably more stringent approach towards the European Community.

Chancellor Schmidt was not especially happy at the first news of the Brussels agreement. It appeared that Herr Klaus von Dohnanyi, the Minister of State at the German Foreign Office, had gone beyond his negotiating brief in terms of the settlement offered, and there was distinct irritation at the Ministry of Finance, which would have to find the money. Of course, the government accepted the agreement in the end, but it also made clear that there were limits to German largesse. Herr von Dohnanyi said afterwards that if the Community had broken up over the budget contributions, 'it would no longer have been able to tackle the urgent question of agricultural reform'. The Federal government insisted not only that agricultural spending must be reformed, but also that it must be done within the Community's existing agreed resources.

An official statement on 4 June 1980 read in part:

The Federal Government confirms with emphasis the need expressed in the EEC agreements for existing imbalances in the Community budget to be evened out at source by structural changes. It also underlines the necessity that the EEC Commission should propose before 1 June 1981 effective measures to cut down farm surpluses so that the increase in agricultural expenditure can be kept below the increase in the Community's own receipts.

In other words, there was a specific commitment to reform of the conduct of the agricultural policy which could not be judged simply by increasing Community resources so that more money could be spent for non-agricultural purposes while allowing the present level of spending on agriculture to continue.

To make that clear beyond doubt, the statement went on: 'The Federal government adheres firmly to the opinion that in the future too the VAT contribution to the EEC should not exceed 1 per cent of the agreed basis of calculation.' Those words were quite different from anything said in public by the French. The Germans appeared to be seeking to put a lid on Community expenditure; the French had not explicitly ruled out going beyond the VAT ceiling.

Two other items in the German statement were of

interest. One was the suggestion that a ceiling might have to be placed both on the net contributions to the Community by any individual member and on the amount by which members were allowed to be net beneficiaries. This approach to controlling Community expenditure was believed to have come from Herr Schmidt himself.

The other point in the statement was directed specifically at Britain:

> The Federal government expects the British government to take into proper consideration the interests of EEC fellow-members in pursuing its policies regarding oil and natural gas and in particular the exploitation of its production potential. This should apply especially to supply situations requiring particular Community solidarity.

In short, here was another challenge to the British to do something about energy in a Community context.

There is perhaps a certain irony in the German position on the common agricultural policy, for it has become clear in recent years that the Germans themselves are beneficiaries from it. Far from there being a contract between French agriculture and German industry, the Germans may have learned better than the French how to exploit the CAP. It may be only because the Germans in general are more efficient: it is, after all, quite striking that West Germany is one of the most economically successful states under the capitalist system, while East Germany is one of the most economically successful under the communist system. All the same, German farmers seem to have done rather well. The *Financial Times*, quoting the Central Marketing Organisation for German Agricultural Industries, reported on 26 August 1980 that German food and drink exports to Britain had increased ninefold since the early 1970s and 18 per cent in 1979 alone. The wine may be one thing, but Britain did not exactly join the Common Market in order to be able to buy German butter in the supermarket.

There are other instances of the Germans doing better than they ought. Mr Christopher Tugendhat, the EEC Commissioner for budgetary affairs, pointed out as long ago as March 1978 that the lion's share of the Community's agricultural surpluses was held in Germany. On the European Commission's own figures, 73 per cent of the Community's butter stocks were held in Germany in April 1978, and 67 per cent of skimmed milk powder stocks. These are usually the two main surplus products, and the German element in the surplus was steadily rising. So was Germany's share of agricultural exports. The French share of Community agricultural exports was at best static. It was the Germans who accounted for the bulk of the rise in the Community's agricultural spending.

It is said that there was a political excuse: Chancellor Schmidt was dependent on his small coalition partner, the Free Democrat Party, which was in turn dependent on the votes of Bavarian farmers. Among British officials there was a slightly different gloss: it was suggested that the CAP simply enabled the part-time Bavarian farmer to buy his fourth Mercedes, and certainly Bavarian smallholdings had a marked degree of affluence. Chancellor Schmidt may have wanted reform of the CAP and been merely biding his time until after the elections, but he has shown no great inclination to push it through, except by demanding a clampdown on expenditure in general.

After the German elections Herr Josef Ertl, the Free Democrat Minister of Agriculture, continued to hold the post that he has held since 1969. Herr Ertl is a Bavarian and has been a formidable opponent of reform of the CAP. At least at the top, Franco-German relations continued to be as close as ever. The meeting between Chancellor Schmidt and President Giscard in Paris in February 1981

was the 37th Franco-German summit in the last 15 years
or so. That fact alone is enough to make one wonder
whether Britain can ever get inside the Bonn–Paris alliance.
French decision-making, however, went into abeyance
because of the approach of the elections at home.

There turned out to be a certain irony in President
Giscard's statement in January: 'France is about to enter
a period in which she will be unable to make proposals,
since her political activity will be suspended by the normal
democratic deadline of her presidential election.' As
already noted, he lost. But the statement was still broadly
true. The new French government *may* turn out to be
more *communautaire* and M Cheysson has spoken of going
beyond the bilateral Franco–German relationship to take
more account of the wishes of the rest of the Community.
We shall see.

At any rate, the scene is now set for serious negotiations
on the future of the Community. For the sake of delineat-
ing the argument, it is worth setting out both a minimalist
and a maximalist position for the Community as a whole,
though of course in reality there are all sorts of positions
in between.

The minimalist approach would be to accept the 1 per
cent VAT barrier on Community spending and to seek to
restructure the Community budget within that limit: more
money might go on regional and social policies, for
example, and less on agriculture. The enlargement of the
Community would have to be accommodated without any
great increase in Community outlays. At the same time,
there might be a concerted effort to create a genuine Common Market by eliminating non-tariff barriers to trade.
The French, for instance, might be asked to be less resist-
ant to takeover bids by companies inside the Community.
There might also be more competition for public sector

contracts between one member country and another. None of that would be negligible. Moreover, there is no obvious reason why it should not be compatible with further progress towards political cooperation, nor towards further *ad hoc* cooperation in other fields such as high technology and energy.

The maximalist or grand approach would consist of accepting the Community as dynamic. It would not preclude, indeed it would require, reform of the CAP, nor would it stick at the present expenditure limits. Instead it would look for new ways of transferring Community resources towards the poorer members, especially in the light of enlargement. Spain and Portugal, after all, are poor in a way that does not apply to Britain. They might reasonably expect some financial benefit from joining that goes beyond the elimination of tariff barriers. A more dynamic Community would also seek to develop a common energy policy and deliberately to promote its interdependence rather than simply react to events. European unity, in short, would be taken as the fundamental starting point rather than a fallback position. Political cooperation would become a keystone, something to be deliberately pursued, rather than regarded as incidental, and deserving of a treaty in its own right.

For Britain the choice is more difficult than for the other members, though it should be remembered that the choice is facing them all. Britain is in this respect an equal partner. But as indicated in the first two chapters, Britain and perhaps Denmark are the only two countries even to have contemplated withdrawal. The Community could go on without them. The British have increasingly to be convinced of the merits of staying in. It will be argued in the rest of this book that both Britain and Europe would benefit more from the maximalist approach. The three areas chosen for discussion, and which necessarily overlap, are political cooperation, resource transfer, and energy policy.

CHAPTER 4

Political Cooperation

Over the past 20 years or so the balance of power in the world has changed substantially. It is not just what is sometimes called the 'central balance' between the United States and the Soviet Union, though that too has changed almost beyond recognition. There have also been changes in the balance between Western Europe and the US and within Western Europe itself.

Not least, there are new centres of commercial if not military power. Twenty years ago, for example, who foresaw the rise of the Japanese export machine, first in motorcars, then in electronics and now perhaps in telematics? There are also new sources of instability. The Middle East was always considered important, but became even more so once the oil producers discovered the 'oil weapon' of raising oil prices and limiting supplies. Crises can arise, such as the Iran—Iraq war in 1979, which the superpowers are unable to control, either together or separately. Even Saudi Arabia, long viewed in the West as the guardian of secure oil supplies, and as holding some power of veto over the price, is considered by the experts to be distinctly vulnerable to internal upheaval.

That is a broad 20-year perspective, to which we shall return. But here is also a ten-year perspective which is no more encouraging. The early 1970s were generally thought to be the 'era of negotiations'. There was the first strategic arms limitation treaty (SALT I) between the US and the Soviet Union, the West German *Ostpolitik,* and the treaties between West Germany and Poland and between West Germany and the Russians. Not all of this progress was purely bilateral. The major Western allies and the Russians negotiated the four-power agreement on Berlin. More multilateral still, East and West began talks in Vienna on mutually balanced force reductions (MBFR) in Central Europe. All European states except Albania, plus the US and Canada, finally reached agreement at the Conference on Security and Cooperation in Europe (CSCE) which culminated in the signing of the Final Act in Helsinki in 1975.

What was happening was an attempt if not to end East-West confrontation, at least to contain it. Behind the arms control agreements and the German treaties, there was also a desire for greater East-West trade and — at least on the Western side — an implicit assumption that that itself would lessen confrontation. The Soviet attitude towards West Germany, for example, began to change dramatically from early 1969 onwards. It is possible to argue that it altered because the Russians foresaw the coming to power of a Social Democrat-led government, as indeed happened later that year. (The first sign of the Kremlin's change of approach came when red roses were sent to mark the election of the Social Democrat, Dr Gustav Heinemann, as President of the Federal Republic on 5 March 1969.) There may be something in that, but it is much more likely that the Soviet leadership came to realise that it had nothing to gain from keeping such a key economic power as West Germany had become on near-enemy terms. In any case, Soviet policy changed from one of regarding the Federal Republic as basically revanchiste to one of seeking commercial partnership.

Practically all the agreements sought in the early 1970s

were worthwhile in their own right, at least in principle. But it soon became clear that they had limitations. It was not possible to have a code for East-West behaviour in Europe, and to expect that East-West relations would therefore be more harmonious in the rest of the world. There was no code of behaviour elsewhere. The Helsinki Final Act did not prevent the Soviet invasion of Afghanistan, nor is there any evidence that the Russians regarded the Act as an impediment when they contemplated intervening directly in Poland after the rise of the free trade union movement, Solidarity.

The agreements of the early 1970s also did nothing to prevent the growth of Soviet military power. It is significant that the one negotiation that might have led to a measure of arms control in central Europe — the MBFR talks in Vienna — got nowhere. So much for the original idea of using MBFR to give a military dimension to détente: that is, to provide the military counterpart to the Helsinki Agreement.

In retrospect, it can be seen that the negotiations of the 1970s were tied to the world of the 1960s, or perhaps even earlier. They assumed if not that the world was Eurocentric, at least that there was some straight East-West balance which would tend to help resolve other problems if it could be held. Yet the genie was already out of the bottle. In SALT, for example, the technology was moving faster than the diplomacy. The first SALT agreement did not cover multiple independently-targetable re-entry vehicles (MIRVs) because the Russians did not have them at the time. It became clear that it was a very inadequate agreement when the Russians caught up with the MIRV technology: the SALT treaty put a ceiling on the number of delivery vehicles, but not on the number of warheads.

There was the same dilemma in Europe, and it is here that the 20-year and the ten-year perspectives come together. The Soviet Union had long been seeking to extend its power beyond the European continent. The Cuban missile crisis, which showed a Soviet desire to reach way outside the traditional sphere of influence, took place as early as 1962. Indeed it seems likely that it was the eventual Soviet rebuff in Cuba which led to the Kremlin's decision to develop naval power on a worldwide basis – with air support where necessary. Historically Russia had always been a land power. At any rate, by the early 1970s the idea of dealing with the Soviet Union only in Europe had become unrealistic.

There were also more gradual changes in Western Europe. France, it is true, had always had claims to being a world power. But in the late 1960s and early 1970s the most striking change was in West Germany. In the 1960s the Federal Republic was not even a member of the United Nations, despite having one of the most powerful economies in the world: the phrase used by Herr Willy Brandt when he was Foreign Minister was that the country was 'an economic giant, but a political pygmy'. Its relations with Moscow tended to be conducted through the major Western powers, mainly America. By the early 1970s, however, West Germany was politically altogether more active: not only through the *Ostpolitik,* but also through the development of the relationship with France and an increasing tendency to stand up to the US.

These changes in the balance of power within the Western alliance are worth pursuing further, for they are of fundamental importance to Britain's foreign policy options. They can be best seen perhaps in economic terms, though these have a great deal to do with what ultimately becomes politics. The starkest example is again West Germany. In the 1970s the dollar halved its value against the D-mark. Currency developments in the Federal Republic have a wider following, at least until recently, than those in Britain. The D-mark/dollar movement over the years was seen as – and indeed was – itself a change in the balance of power.

It was the Germans who were shoring up the American currency, and the Germans noticed. So, too, did some Americans. In the industrial field it was the Germans who went into America and set up their own car production facilities. Volkswagen of America will probably shortly become the third largest car-producing company in the US, after General Motors and Ford. That is a far cry from the days when it seemed that Europe was being swamped by American investment and superior American technology. The so-called 'technology gap' between Europe and the US hardly exists any more. The mainly Franco—German Airbus consortium, once shunned by the British, now sells more civil aircraft than any company except Boeing.

There have also been the changes in France. Who could have thought only a few years ago – let alone 20 years – that it would be the French company Peugeot that would buy up the European end of Chrysler? A far more likely guess was that the purchase would be the other way round. That is a perfect example of the change in the balance of power.

It is impossible to separate what has happened in the economic-industrial area from the political-strategic. When John Kennedy became American President 20 years ago, he called for a 'twin pillar' relationship between Europe and the US: the alternative phrase used was 'dumb-bells', implying a balance between more or less equal partners. In fact, such a relationship was inconceivable at the time. Europe lacked the self-confidence, both economic and political, to behave as anything like an equal. It also lacked the means. The US then was incomparably more powerful *vis-à-vis* both the Soviet Union and Western Europe than it is today. At that time it was *the* superpower.

Yet today the conditions for a twin pillar relationship exist. Europe and the US are broadly economic equals. Europe no longer has an inferiority complex about American technology. There is also a political maturity. The Europeans both expect and in fact do have a say in

East-West relations and in dealings with the rest of the world. They conduct their own bilateral, sometimes multilateral diplomacy. Quite often they disagree with the Americans.

But there is one crucial difference between the Europe of today and the Europe that was envisaged by some early supporters of the European Community. Whereas it was sometimes thought that Europe would have to strike off on its own, away from the US, the Europe that has developed seeks only partnership. It would be very difficult to imagine more Atlanticist leaders in France and Germany than Valéry Giscard d'Estaing and Helmut Schmidt, who had such a close understanding for much of the 1970s. France and Germany do not seek an independent defence community. On the contrary, they want closer Atlantic relations. It was very striking that one of the first acts of President Mitterrand was to send the French foreign minister to Washington to provide reassurance that the France—American relations would remain close. According to all US sources, M Cheysson's visit was a great success.

The Europeans have recognised that the idea of an independent European nuclear deterrent — to be operated as if the US did not exist — is not credible. West Germany, after all, could not acquire nuclear weapons overnight, even if it wished to try. Imagine the Soviet — and other — reactions if it were to attempt it! Europe is not strong enough to stand up to the Soviet Union alone. It is even less capable of standing up to the Soviet Union outside the European continent. It therefore needs, and recognises that it needs, the American partnership.

For the first time, there are the glimmerings of a belief that this partnership must go beyond the defence of Europe. The French have seen this more readily than the Germans. Indeed one of the ironies of the last few years is that relations between Washington and Paris are now closer than those between Washington and Bonn. One explanation is simply that President Carter and Chancellor Schmidt never got on: the Carter administration was deeply suspicious of all things German and had no experts on Germany in its entourage. The Germans also disliked being lectured on human rights.

A more profound explanation, however, is that the Germans felt that they had come of age by joining, even leading, the mainstream of East-West European negotiations in the early 1970s, and were not yet ready to move on to a wider stage. Besides, German involvement outside Europe might have endangered the gains of the *Ostpolitik*: hence the relatively restrained German reaction to the Soviet invasion of Afghanistan, though the Germans did join the Americans in boycotting the 1980 Moscow Olympics. The French, by contrast, have maintained a more jaundiced view of Soviet intentions. (Innate suspicion of the Soviet Union seems even stronger in the Quai d'Orsay than it is in the British Foreign Office.) They have had no intellectual difficulties in seeking to respond to possible Soviet advances outside Europe. In the Iran—Iraq war it was almost a matter of course that the French should increase their naval presence in the Gulf and the Indian Ocean. The Americans were appreciative. Indeed stories of the French not pulling their weight within the Atlantic alliance now belong either to the press or the past. On defence expenditure the French have been expanding faster than both the British and the Germans. Nothing that was said in M Mitterrand's election campaign suggested any lessening of the French effort.

Still, the Germans too have been moving. It was Herr Hans Apel, the German Defence Minister, who proposed early in 1980 that there should be a new 'division of labour' within the alliance. The German contribution was to be increased aid to Turkey, and to some extent to Pakistan. Before that it was Chancellor Schmidt himself who took the lead in calling for a Western response to the new

Soviet missiles — the SS-20s — targeted on Western Europe, and who successfully defended the American decision to base cruise missiles in Europe in the face of strong opposition from his own Social Democrat Party. One may also wonder if the West Germany of the 1960s or even early 1970s would have undertaken the rescue of the German hostages in Mogadishu in 1977. It was the first time that the Federal Republic had been engaged in military action outside Europe. Herr Schmidt said that the participants were not soldiers but policemen, and in fact the rescue was internationally coordinated, with the British SAS playing a part. But for the Germans to go into Africa at all was a notable departure. The risk for the German government was very large: it is worth thinking what the consequences might have been if the rescue attempt had failed. The Federal Chancellor would have almost certainly been obliged to resign.

Of course, it might be said that what I have been writing about is the relationship between France and Germany, and that this could operate even without the European Community. Perhaps it could. Yet the fact remains that the French and the Germans take the Community for granted. They operate within it when possible and outside it when necessary. It is doubtful whether they would take kindly to a country which, having been in the Community and then rejected it, still sought to continue foreign policy cooperation.

The problem for Britain is really this. A new power centre has arisen in France and Germany, who happen to be the leading memebers of the Community. The US has grown relatively weaker. So, too, has Britain. So how does Britain best try to exercise what power and influence it might still have? The idea of the special relationship with the US is out, despite a certain ideological similarity between Mrs Thatcher and President Reagan. Britain is simply too weak to be an adequate partner. Besides, it is no longer a British Prime Minister who goes to Moscow to initiate key international negotiations such as the partial test ban treaty. It is more likely to be Chancellor Schmidt. The Americans and the Russians are as aware of this change in the balance of power within Europe as anyone else. The new power centre has become a reality.

That does not mean that Britain has nothing to contribute. Far from it. There are parts of the world where British experience is considerable and the British reputation still high, but where we are too weak economically and militarily to act alone. The Gulf and the Middle East are obvious examples. So are large parts of Africa. Yet Britain is not unique in this. The same might be said of France. Even West Germany has areas where it appears to be especially appreciated. Turkey is one, but there are also strong German connections throughout Eastern Europe. It is therefore a question of pooling the knowledge and the experience and seeking to act together.

M Henri Simonet, the former Belgian Foreign Minister, once said that if the European Community had a foreign policy, everyone would know. That is a measure of how far there is to go. Yet the machinery for improved foreign policy cooperation does exist and goes back over a decade. In Britain it has never been much publicised, even until recently by pro-Marketeers. The only full set of published texts relating to European political cooperation (Poco for short) comes from the Press and Information Office of the German government. British diplomats needing to look up the original Poco texts tend to fall back on the English translation provided by the Germans. So far as I have been able to discover, there has been only one book on the subject, the largely descriptive *La Coopération politique européenne* (Editions LABOR, 1980), by the Belgian diplomat M Philippe de Schoutheete.

This is such a peculiar lacuna that it is worth giving some space to saying that Poco is — and what it is not.

First of all, it has nothing to do with the Treaty of Rome. That Treaty is about the creation of an economic community. It moves into foreign affairs largely because a common commercial policy implies a uniform approach to third countries. The power to negotiate trading agreements with outside parties is of course a considerable one to give to the Brussels Commission, and has been largely responsible for much of the rest of the world believing that the Community is more powerful than it really is. But it has little to do with foreign policy in the traditional sense.

Poco came later. Its origins go back to the summit meeting of the original six members of the Community in The Hague in December 1969. The entire Hague communiqué indeed repays re-reading, because it is a reminder of how high the sights then were. It was the Hague summit, for instance, that agreed on the system of 'own resources' which now largely finances the Community budget. It also agreed that a phased plan should be worked out during 1970 'with a view to the creation of an economic and monetary union'. Not least, it called for the further co-ordination and promotion of industrial research and development, and promised to supply the financial means for that purpose.

For our subject, however, it is paragraph 15 that matters, whereby heads of state and government 'agreed to instruct the Ministers of State for Foreign Affairs to study the best way of achieving progress in the matter of political unification, within the context of enlargement. The Ministers would be expected to report before the end of July 1970.'

The Community in those days moved fast. What became known as the Luxembourg Report was approved and published on 27 October 1970. There is a good deal in the document that will not appeal to every British ear: for example, the references to the need for Europe 'to show the whole world' that it has a 'political mission'. Yet the Luxembourg Report is also the first basic text laying down the aims and methods of foreign policy cooperation. 'The present development of the European Communities,' it says, 'requires member states to intensify their political cooperation and provide in an initial phase the mechanism for harmonising their views regarding international affairs'. The objectives of the member states are defined as follows:

> to ensure, through regular changes of information and consultations, a better mutual understanding on the great international problems;
> to strengthen their solidarity by promoting the harmonisation of their views, the coordination of their positions, and, where it appears possible and desirable, common actions.

It was arranged that the foreign ministers should meet at least every six months. (In fact, the first ministerial meeting under Poco took place in Munich less than one month after the publication of the Luxembourg Report: the European Security Conference and the Middle East were on the agenda.) Ministers could be replaced by heads of state or government if it was felt that circumstances warranted it. In the event of a crisis, there would be extraordinary consultations between member states.

The Report also went into some of the backup arrangements. The ministerial meetings were to be prepared by a committee composed of the directors of political affairs – senior diplomats in the national Foreign Offices who, at least in principle, have access to all departments. These political directors were themselves to meet at least four times a year, both to prepare the ministerial sessions and to carry out any special tasks that ministers might delegate. They were empowered to set up working groups to deal with particular problems and to appoint groups of experts to give advice.

Under the heading 'subjects for Consultation', the
Luxembourg Report says simply:

Governments will consult on all important questions
of foreign policy.

Member states may propose any question of their
choice for political consultation.

Not content with all that, however, the document also laid
down that there should be further studies on 'the best way
of achieving progress in the field of political unification'. A
second report was promised.

Political cooperation was meanwhile under way. The
Paris Summit in October 1972 was another of those
occasions, this time with the British in attendance — prior
to joining the Community in January the next year, which
reminds us how ambitious the heads of government used
to be. The communiqué spoke of an 'irreversible determination' to achieve economic and monetary union. It also
broke new ground in declaring that 'high priority' should
be given to the aim of correcting structural and regional
balances within the Community, and invited the Community institutions to set up a Regional Development
Fund to be financed from the Community's own resources
within the next 12 months — this reflects the influence of
the British Primine Minister, Mr Heath. It called for the
establishment of a 'single industrial base' for the Community as a whole, and the final paragraph confirmed the
(undefined) aim of European Union by the end of the
decade. (The Paris communiqué is also notable for a brief
reference to energy policy. It was deemed necessary to
'invite the Community Institutions to formulate as soon as
possible an energy policy guaranteeing certain and lasting
supplies under satisfactory economic conditions'. That was
before the energy crisis of 1973. Some people might say
that the Community has not moved much since.)

Still, it is political cooperation that concerns us here. The Paris communiqué said that the process had begun well and should be further improved. The foreign ministers were instructed in future to meet four times a year instead of twice, wearing their Poco hats. The Paris summit also agreed that the aim of political cooperation was 'to deal with problems of current interest and, where possible, to formulate common medium- and long-term positions'. That latter phrase was a significant advance on the language of the Luxembourg Report. Finally, the summit reminded the foreign ministers of their promise to produce a second report on developing political cooperation.

It was this second report — otherwise known as the Copenhagen Report, of July 1973 — which effectively laid the basis of political cooperation as it has been practised until the present day. It introduced a number of practical improvements. The political directors were instructed to meet as often as the intensification of their work required. A new group was set up consisting of European '*Correspondants*'. These were more junior but not necessarily less bright diplomats than the political directors. They had the task of coordinating a great deal of the work. The Copenhagen Report also encouraged the idea of bringing together the senior officials of the national foreign ministries for regular contacts even if there was no pressing subject to discuss. It was assumed that it would be natural and desirable for them to have views and information to exchange.

There were several new dimensions. Members of the Community were instructed to appoint a member of their diplomatic staff in their embassies in other Community countries, to be responsible for ensuring the necessary contacts with the local foreign ministry on anything that had to do with political cooperation. Embassies of member states in third countries were told to keep in much closer touch with each other than in the past. Perhaps most important of all, the permanent representatives of the member states to the major international organisations — which include the OECD, the UN and NATO — were asked regularly to consider matters together and 'on the basis on instructions received' to seek common positions.

One notable innovation was the decision to facilitate better communications between the Community's foreign ministries. A special telex link was established, dispatching what are called 'Coreus' (short for *correspondant européen*). Not long afterwards, Coreus were running at several thousand a year.

The Copenhagen Report was also more specific about the priorities in the matters to be dealt with under political cooperation. On this it is worth quoting in full. The relevant section runs:

> Governments will consult each other on all important foreign policy questions and will work out priorities, observing the following criteria:
> the purpose of the consultation is to seek common policies on practical problems;
> the subject dealt with must concern European interests whether in Europe itself or elsewhere where the adoption of a common policy is either necessary or desirable.
>
> On these questions each state undertakes as a general rule not to take up final positions without prior consultation with its partners within the framework of the political cooperation machinery.

There is nothing final, nothing in any way contractually binding. Note the insertion of that phrase 'as a general rule' in the section about the commitment to prior consultation. The let-out is certainly there. Nevertheless, the document does read like a pretty close acceptance of the idea of foreign policy cooperation wherever possible. What is more, it went a long way towards establishing the machinery that would implement that cooperation.

Two other developments ought to be mentioned. The first is the Document on the European Identity published by the nine foreign ministers of the enlarged Community in Copenhagen in December 1973, and the second is what is known as the Gymnich formula.

The Document on the European Identity is in many ways embarrassing to read, especially for the British. It offends British pragmatism. If there is such a thing as a 'European identity', the British would tend to say, there is surely no need to write it down because everybody would know what it is. Besides, it had long been a British article of faith that the British and European identities were quite separate. That was what British history was about. And it is true that the tone is self-conscious and smacks of that mysticism about Europe which has so offended British people who would otherwise support membership of the Community on purely practical grounds. Still, the Document is worth attention. It begins:

> The Nine Member Countries of the European Communities have decided that the time has come to draw up a document on the European Identity. This will enable them to achieve a better definition of their relations with other countries and of their responsibilities and the place which they occupy in world affairs. They have decided to define the European Identity with the dynamic nature of the Community in mind. They have the intention of carrying the work further in the future in the light of the progress made in the construction of a United Europe.

Defining the European Identity involved (and here an element of mysticism creeps in): 'Reviewing the common heritage, interests and special obligations of the Nine, as

well as the degree of unity so far achieved within the Com-
r unity.' It is the idea of there being a 'common heritage'
that clearly sticks in some British throats. Yet there were
also some straightforward even pragmatic statements
which are equally valid today. For example:

> Although in the past the European countries were
> individually able to play a major role on the inter-
> national scene, present international problems are
> difficult for any of the Nine to solve alone. Inter-
> national developments and the growing concentration
> of power and responsibility in the hands of a very
> small number of great powers mean that Europe must
> unite and speak increasingly with one voice if it wants
> to make itself heard and play its proper role in the
> world.

There was, too, an element of realism. The Document
said: 'The Nine, one of whose essential aims is to maintain
peace, will never succeed in doing so if they neglect their
own security.' Then it added: 'Those of them who are
members of the Atlantic Alliance consider that in present
circumstances there is no alternative to the security provided by the nuclear weapons of the United States and by
the presence of North American forces in Europe.' No
nonsense there about the need to break with the US in
order to establish European independence.

One final section deserves quoting, not because it is
particularly profound but because it seems to me to be
true and indeed to be the essence of what the European
Community is about:

> European unification is not directed against anyone,
> nor is it inspired by a desire for power. On the con-
> trary, the Nine are convinced that their union will
> benefit the whole international community since it

will constitute an element of equilibrium and a basis of cooperation with all countries, whatever their size, culture or social system.

Looking back, the Document on the European Identity can be seen as marking the end of an era. Not that it was wrong; rather it was stillborn, or overtaken by events. The Copenhagen Summit, of which it was part, was an unhappy affair. The Middle East war of October 1973 and the use of the oil weapon by the oil-producing states had removed the old certainties. The postwar period of sustained economic growth was at an end. Never since has Europe sought to speak in such grandiose language. It is a point worth noting that Britain joined the EEC at a time when Europe had run out of steam, not so much because of its own failings but because of the pressure of outside events over which it had little or no control. After 1973 the Community became an altogether more modest endeavour, doing its best to avoid going backwards rather than talking about schemes for political union by the end of the decade.

None the less, the groundwork for political cooperation had at least been completed, and the events of 1973 did lead to one further significant development. This was the Gymnich formula.

Among other things, the Middle East war severely strained US-European relations. Dr Henry Kissinger, then the US Secretary of State, had been complaining for some time that there was no one representing Europe with whom the US could speak. The Europeans had themselves been complaining about the failure of the Americans to hold proper consultations with their transatlantic allies. Thus in June 1974 the foreign ministers of the Nine met informally at Schloss Gymnich near Bonn and agreed on a new procedural approach. It was established that whoever held the presidency of the Community could consult or inform outside powers about the deliberations held under political cooperation. (The presidency rotates between member states on a six-monthly basis.) Thus if, for example, the foreign ministers had been discussing the Middle East, the foreign minister of the country which held the presidency at the time might inform interested parties of what had been said. Informal meetings of the kind held at Schloss Gymnich also became a regular part of the political cooperation procedure.

There have been no substantial changes in the mechanics of political cooperation, though there have been some operational refinements since. It has become part of a European foreign minister's way of life. In 1973, for instance, M Michel Jobert, the French Foreign Minister at the time, insisted that Poco and the Treaty of Rome were so separate that ministers and officials could not meet in the same place on the same day to do the business of both. On one famous occasion ministers met in Copenhagen in the morning wearing their Common Market hats; the French saw to it that they were then flown to Brussels to get on with their Poco business in the afternoon. That sort of nonsense now belongs to the past. Foreign policy cooperation is frequently discussed on the fringe of Council of Ministers' meetings.

Yet how has Poco developed over the years? The conventional answer from diplomats is that the member states have indeed drawn a great deal closer together in the making of foreign policy. At the United Nations prior consultations among the Nine became a matter of course: quite frequently the state which holds the presidency of the Community now speaks on behalf of all its members before the General Assembly. A minor landmark was passed when the Soviet delegate, who had originally derided the whole idea of the Nine acting together, one day demanded to know what the Community thought.

There are other examples of close cooperation. The

most obvious is the approach to the Conference on Security and Cooperation in Europe, not only in the original negotiations leading to the Helsinki Agreement but also in the two follow-up conferences in Belgrade and Madrid. The Nine went out of their way to coordinate their positions. Often, as at the United Nations, this cooperation continued at the diplomatic level even when the Nine foreign ministers were quarrelling about quite different matters.

If one wants a specific case where Poco directly helped the British, it has to be Rhodesia. The British were able to explain through Poco precisely what they were trying to do to bring about an independent Zimbabwe. Rhodesia was regarded by the Europeans as a largely British preserve. If it had not been for the political cooperation forum, it is quite likely that there would have been a great deal of European competition for influence in that part of Africa, and the British motives might have seemed suspect, even colonialist. As it was, European — and American — policy was coordinated. The Europeans were informed about what was going on in a way that could never have happened at the time of the unilateral declaration of Rhodesian independence in 1965, and they respected the British achievement.

The most contentious area considered under political cooperation is the Middle East, if only for the obvious reason that the Europeans have influence but very little power. It has been a long slow process, and there have been frequent fears — sometimes realised — that European and American lines could become crossed. Yet it is a fact that Europe has an experience of the region that has not been shared by the US.

It was the French who first saw the dangers to the West arising from apparently uncritical support for Israel. General de Gaulle changed his position on Israel and became more sympathetic to the Arab states ahead of

French public opinion and ahead of most European leaders. It was also the French who first pointed to the possibility of an energy crisis as a result of Middle East turbulence. Since then, the Community has gradually evolved a position of recognising the rights of the Palestinians and the Israelis to live within secure, recognised and guaranteed borders. There has been no question of negotiations with the parties involved, since Europe has no power on its own to deliver, but direct contacts have steadily increased. President Giscard commented in December 1980 that the document produced by M Gaston Thorn, then the Luxembourg Foreign Minister, who had been holding talks in the Middle East on behalf of the Community, was among the most comprehensive and detailed ever produced. Future developments awaited the development of a Middle East policy by the new American administration, but at least it looked as if Europe had done its homework.

Yet the fact remains that political cooperation is a curiously unsung achievement. The Luxembourg and Copenhagen Reports are virtually unknown outside a small circle. The Document on the European Identity is remembered with a flicker of embarrassment by those who recall it at all. Why this should be so is a question for the diplomats and the foreign ministers. The diplomats say that it is not their business to seek publicity. The foreign ministers say that Poco is all very well, and is nowadays taken for granted by the practitioners, but that it has its limitations.

Indeed it has. It should be said at first that a degree of European foreign policy cooperation would almost surely have developed in any case even without the framework laid down by the Luxembourg and Copenhagen Reports. It is inconceivable that there could have been agreement on the Helsinki Final Act, for instance, without the closest consultations between West European capitals. In fact, the European neutrals, not to speak of the non-Common Market members of NATO, were also closely involved, so it is incorrect to regard Helsinki on the Western side as specifically an achievement of the Nine. Western Europe also shares common interests at the United Nations which have often compelled it to vote as a bloc. It would therefore be unwise to attribute to political cooperation what might have happened without the formal procedures for consultation.

There are also structural weaknesses. None of the texts relating to political cooperation lays down that there should be a common foreign policy. At best, they prepare the way for the member states to coordinate their national foreign policies, though even here there are always let-outs. There is something arbitrary about what is discussed. So far as is known the Spanish Sahara, which does actually involve a war not too far from Europe, has never been mentioned. From the British point of view, neither has Gibraltar, nor the problems of Northern Ireland: perhaps thankfully, perhaps not.

Even where the Luxembourg Report did make provision for extraordinary consultations in the event of an emergency, it is notable that when the Soviet Union invaded Afghanistan in late 1979 — admittedly it was Christmas time — nothing happened. The machinery failed to work or, to be more accurate, the people concerned failed to use it. Nevertheless, perhaps the failure helped to concentrate the mind. The Soviet intervention in Afghanistan subsequently became one of the main themes of Poco discussions.

There is still no fixed organisation. Political cooperation tends to be run by whichever member state happens to hold the presidency at a particular time. True, there have been certain minor innovations over the years. The country giving up the presidency seconds a member of its diplomatic staff who has worked on political cooperation to the country taking over. A diplomat from the country which will take over the presidency after that is also seconded. A certain amount of continuity is thus assured. But the real reason for this (fairly limited) device was a concern on the part of the larger members that the smaller members of the Community might be unable to cope with holding the presidency on their own. No one (I hope) has anything against Ireland or indeed Luxembourg, nor against the quality of their diplomatic services. But if the Community foreign ministers have been having a discussion about South Africa and then something needs to be communicated, face to face, to Pretoria, there is a question whether the smaller countries have the resources to cope.

There is a recurrent idea that there should be a permanent secretariat. Lord Carrington, the British Foreign Secretary, revived it, though without using that particular term, in a speech in Hamburg in November 1980. Yet the issues of where it should be based — if it should be permanently based at all — and what precisely it should do, have still to be faced.

Still, it was a breakthrough of a kind that Lord Carrington should have made the Hamburg speech that he did. The Foreign Secretary was reflecting some of the thinking that had been going on inside the British government about how the Community could best work after the interim agreement on the British contribution to the budget. The development of political cooperation is as good a way as any for the British to shape a Community to their own liking. It does not cost any money. It is an area where Britain with its worldwide experience has considerable influence and respect. Moreover, closer foreign policy cooperation in Western Europe will have to happen in any case. It is the only way in which Europe can effectively talk to the Americans, the Japanese, the Russians, the oil producers and the Third World. The alternatives are European dissension and — for the British — a decision to drop out of the mainstream of international developments in the mistaken belief that it is possible to stop the world and get off.

Ideally, the next step should be to draw up an equivalent to the Luxembourg and Copenhagen Reports, suited to the world of the 1980s, and acknowledging that Europe is now more than a fledgling entity in international affairs. It would accept that political cooperation under the existing agreements has probably already reached the limits of the possible: there is simply no time to hold more and more meetings, when both ministers and officials are already overburdened. Instead the new report would call for the establishment of the permanent (but small) secretariat which would service the foreign ministers on a continuing basis.

Above all, there would have to be some greater link than there is today between the traditional idea of foreign policy and what actually happens in interstate relations. The idea of the European Community delivering a note to South Africa over pay for black workers or to the Turkish government for its attitude to Cyprus is all very well, except that everybody knows that the Community has little power to back its words. Foreign policy today is much more about the awarding of contracts, export credits and perhaps trade sanctions. The parts of the Community which deal with external trade policy and with foreign policy in the traditional sense need to be brought together. They are often the very same people, simply wearing different hats.

Take just one example: it might concern Poland, or indeed Eastern Europe in general. What has been happening in Poland since the rise of the Solidarity movement is clearly of considerable significance to the rest of Europe and beyond. The Polish situation has been discussed under Poco. Yet there is also a Community commercial policy towards Poland. It would be comforting to know that the purely foreign policy considerations — if it is any longer possible to speak in those terms — have been discussed alongside the commercial considerations. For instance, if the Community foreign ministers were to decide that a Soviet intervention in Eastern Europe warranted economic sanctions against the Soviet Union, how could they ensure that their decision was put into effect by the Community as a whole? What would they do about existing contracts? How would they square the ministries of trade or economics? How would they know about the legal position of companies involved in East-West trade?

What we know about the present machinery suggests that there would be some confusion, to put it mildly. Nobody knows how far political cooperation is supposed to go, or how far it can go. Nobody knows either what the relationship between political cooperation and the Community as laid down by the Treaty of Rome is supposed to be. Poco as it has developed is excessively pragmatic, even by British standards.

There is one important corollary to the idea of the permanent secretariat. It would have to have high-level access not only to the foreign ministries but to every government department. If one thing has become clear over the years, it is that you cannot make a policy for Europe by means of foreign ministries alone. Agriculture, the treasury, trade, industry, the environment, all those ministries have to come in, and the secretariat would need powers to consult with all of them. One way of facilitating that would be to second civil servants from these other ministries to the secretariat. The result might be the nucleus of a machine that could help the Community to see its way in the world.

Some people may see this as an approach to European federalism by other means. Others might see it as a way to get round the Treaty of Rome. My own view, for what it is worth, is that it would be useful for its own sake. If it led down the road to federalism, why not? If it simply meant that increased political cooperation became the main aim of the European Community, that would be a gain in itself. The puzzling question remains why Europe has kept so quiet about the progress of political cooperation so far. The process is already in being, it needs to be developed.

One should not exaggerate. Increased political cooperation would not be a substitute for existing international forums. The degree of cooperation between the major Western powers has actually increased steadily over the last few years: it is a matter of note, for instance, that there have not been greater moves towards economic protectionism. The most effective, and the most private, channel is the Bonn Group consisting of the three Western wartime victors – Britain, France and the US – plus West Germany. Ostensibly, they talk about the situation in and around Berlin. In practice, they talk about anything necessary. (It was the summit meeting of these four in Guadeloupe in early 1979 that decided in principle on the deployment of cruise missiles in Europe.) There are also nowadays the Economic Summits which add Canada, Italy and Japan to the Bonn Group and which by no means confine themselves to matters economic.

A new leap forward in EEC political cooperation would not supplant any of that. Indeed the perennial alliance problem of the smaller countries – Holland, Belgium, Denmark – feeling that they are not sufficiently consulted and are being dragged into great power interests would probably remain. One should not deny that there is an element in what is being suggested here of the old idea of a Political Directorate, consisting of Britain, France, West Germany and possibly Italy. (From the British point of view that would be at least better than the existing directorate of West Germany and France.) Yet greater political cooperation in Europe could offer the best possibility so far of bringing the smaller powers along. The bigger powers would still need to retain their freedom of action in a wider world. Increasingly they would be acting together because of common interests. Europe could go to the most important international meetings – economic, political or both – united.

A sign of movement came from Herr Hans-Dietrich Genscher, the West German Foreign Minister, in a speech to the annual assembly of his Free Democrat Party in Stuttgart on 6 January 1981. Herr Genscher called for a new European Treaty embracing political cooperation. It was a party speech rather than an official German proposal, and it did not go into details, but it is notable that the initial French reaction was not unfavourable and that the Italian response was more than sympathetic. All that should have been the signal for Britain to get off the sidelines.

The fact is that Britain will have to pursue closer political relations with Europe almost regardless of what may happen in the negotiations about strictly Community matters. The change in the balance of power dictates that. There is no longer anywhere else to go. It would be better for Britain to take the lead in a field where it has the experience and the expertise. What about a London Report to go alongside those of Luxembourg and Copenhagen? Or even a Treaty of London to go alongside the Treaty of Rome? It would be the ultimate in missed opportunities if Britain failed to take the initiative when enhanced foreign policy cooperation is now on the agenda.

CHAPTER 5

The Purpose of a Community

The enhanced political cooperation discussed in the previous chapter is something that Britain will almost certainly have to develop in any case, though it will of course be easier in an atmosphere of broadly harmonious relationships with the Community. Barring an outright adoption of protectionism, isolationism, neutralism, or any combination of the three, Europe seems to be the most appropriate forum for Britain to discuss external policy objectives with a view to reaching a consensus that will carry some weight.

The notion is not exclusive, however; no-one is suggesting that bilateral consultations or agreements with other countries should be ruled out. Political cooperation is not intended to be a substitute for other forums that already exist. Indeed its main purpose is to strengthen Europe's voice within those other forums, and it is at least notable that some British politicians who have been sceptical about membership of the Community have appreciated the foreign policy exchanges which Poco allows. Mr James Callaghan, when he was Foreign Secretary, was a conspicuous example of a convert to political cooperation. Even Mr Peter Shore, one of the leading Labour Party anti-

Marketeers, has never attacked the idea of closer European political consultations.

The strengthening of Poco is therefore part of the minimalist approach to reforming the Community. If that was all that Europe was about, one suspects that Britain would have few problems.

The reform of the common agricultural policy is also part of the minimalist approach. By now it should go almost without saying that the CAP has done more than anything else to give the Community a bad name in this country. If it is not reformed, if the surpluses continue to grow and if a seemingly disproportionate amount of Community money continues to be spent on agriculture, then British opposition to membership will go on increasing and will deserve to do so.

Yet it is precisely the point of the Brussels agreement on the British contribution to the Community budget that the resources devoted to agriculture will be limited and that Community expenditure will be restructured. In theory at least, the battle is already won. The negotiations on restructuring may be protracted, but there is already an established ceiling. Within the next year or so Community spending will have reached the maximum allowed under the present arrangements allocating 1 per cent of VAT revenues to the Community's own resources. A British government, if it wanted to, could simply stall until that limit is reached, in the full knowledge that there would then be a Community crisis that would dwarf anything previously known by that name. The Community, in fact, would be close to breaking down under the weight of the CAP's demands.

Things could really go that far, and it is worth remembering that it is within Britain's power to allow it to happen if other members should delay the effort to restructure the budget outlays. It is also worth asking, however, whether there is not a more constructuve approach that goes beyond trying to improve political cooperation and haggling about agricultural policy. In other words, could there not be a more dynamic Community than that which we have grown used to during the period of British membership, or is the British purpose simply to slow down, if not prevent, any development that goes beyond a customs union and a club for discussions about a possible concerted foreign policy?

Here a few general observations are in order. The Community ceased to be dynamic around 1973. The most obvious explanation is that the energy crisis caught it off-balance and unprepared. Continued uncertainty about energy ever since has made it difficult to regain the original sense of progress. The energy crisis more or less coincided with the first enlargement and the advent of what turned out to be a reluctant member, namely Britain. Like Alice in *Through the Looking-Glass,* the Community is sometimes said to have had to run as fast as it can since 1973 in order to stay in the same place. On that score, it has not done too badly. It remains in being, capable of taking off again if it wants to, though the Red Queen's reply to Alice is also pertinent: 'If you want to get somewhere else, you must run at least twice as fast as that.'

Yet the year 1973 or thereabouts would almost certainly have been a turning point in any case. For by then the Community had already achieved many of its main objectives. The customs union was in place. There were imperfections, to be sure, but no one could doubt that the aim of free trade in goods and services, which seemed so ambitious when it was first set, had been largely accomplished. The key question was where to go next.

At the time, and indeed since the late 1960s, the answer seemed to be monetary union. It might even be said that Europe has been littered with (usually abortive) plans for monetary union for the last 15 years. Yet as between the smooth progress towards free trade and the relative failures of the attempts to tie European currencies together, there is one very important distinction that is sometimes forgotten. In the 1960s, the early years of the Community, progress was easy, and this reflected more than just the merits of the Treaty of Rome or the determination of former enemies to work together. What actually happened was that the entire Western international environment was in favour of the reduction of tariff barriers. The period was dominated, in terms of international trade, by the Dillon Round and then the Kennedy Round of tariff cuts. It was also a time of sustained economic expansion. Free – or freer – trade entailed few sacrifices. There were few national constraints when both demand and production were growing. The Community was working with, not against the international grain.

The subsequent attempts at monetary integration were quite different. True, it was becoming increasingly clear that the postwar international monetary system was under serious strain, but it was much less clear that the problems could be resolved by the Community. Certainly there was a case for the member states doing more to help each other: for example, if any of them were in balance of payments difficulties. But the idea that Europe could close itself up and form a monetary bloc on its own was a figment of the European imagination. In retrospect, what the Community should have done was to develop its own thinking on international monetary reform and then discuss them with other key countries and the International Monetary Fund, the IMF. (That is how political cooperation could work at its best.) Instead, Europe devised technical schemes of its own that were almost bound to falter because economic conditions varied so much between one member state and another. Given the varying rates of inflation and of economic growth, it is not surprising that it proved difficult to hold the European exchange rates within fixed bands.

This is a lesson that has taken a long time to learn and may not have been fully learnt even yet. Indeed it is sometimes said that the continuing existence of the present European Monetary System (EMS) is proof to the contrary, and shows that Europe can make its own moves towards monetary integration. There are several answers to this objection. First of all, the system is not Community-wide. Britain is not a member, and the participation of sterling, which has moved from being an exceptionally weak currency to an exceptionally strong one during the EMS lifetime, would have been a far more difficult test. Secondly, there has been a notable reluctance to move beyond the first stage of EMS, which consists of limited support for member currencies, to anything closer to monetary union. Thirdly, and most important, the proponents of EMS have been lucky. The introduction of the system coincided with the recovery of the dollar, so that there were fewer currency upheavals than in the preceding years. There have therefore been fewer strains to withstand, or at least strains of a different kind: the one thing that nobody predicted was that it would be the D-mark which would be among the weaker currencies.

The crucial point, however, is that Europe was at its most successful when it was in tune with the international environment, as when it was developing the customs union. It was much less successful when it sought to strike off on its own, as on monetary integration. With hindsight, the aim of monetary union by 1980 — the objective of the original plans — can be seen as a pipedream. In reality it is doubtful whether it is seriously on the agenda even for 1990. The failure should not distract attention from the lesser but more attainable objective of greater European monetary cooperation. Indeed the sooner the Europeans go to the Americans, the Japanese and the IMF with proposals for international monetary reform the better. There is everything to be said for the Community acting as a kind of pressure group within the international system, and perhaps even acting as a sub- or regional division of the IMF, raising and lending its own funds and exercising its own disciplines. That is what one supposes a Community to be about: forming its own views, putting them into practice wherever possible, and presenting them to the wider world. The cooperation required between European finance ministers and central bankers would simply mirror that required between foreign ministers in the field of foreign policy. It would be part of the natural, minimalist approach towards the development of the Community.

Yet if the customs union is more or less complete and the more ambitious schemes for monetary union have proved unrealistic, are there any new initiatives which the Community could usefully take? One of the peculiarities about the British position in Europe so far is that, when faced with that sort of question, no British government has had anything much to say; nor, if you ask them, have the great majority of senior civil servants outside the Foreign Office. There has been a series of complaints to the effect that the Community works unfairly so far as Britain is concerned, but there has been no alternative British agenda for European development. The British attitude, in short, has been at best passive and at worst negative. The customary question has been: 'What's in it for us?' And the customary answer: 'Not enough!' Perhaps that reflects a more general British malaise. But it is still very striking that it is hard to think of a single significant example of Britain trying to give the Community new dimensions. The overwhelming reaction has been that Europe has too many dimensions already. The British have griped, but they have scarcely put forth remedies except to call for more benefits for themselves. In those circumstances, it is not surprising that Britain has been sometimes viewed as a less than wholehearted member.

In the early 1970s there did seem to be one other

possible new direction for the EEC, apart from the pursuit of monetary union. It concerned the role of public finance, and it may now be worth reviving. In the opening words of the seminal document on the subject, generally known as the MacDougall Report, commissioned in 1974 and published by the EEC in 1977:

> Free trade in goods and services within the Community of Nine has been largely achieved, although significant non-tariff barriers remain in both the industrial and the agricultural fields. Monetary union, on which much has been written, is . . . a long way off and will probably have to await major developments in the political, monetary and fiscal fields. This report examines the third main element in economic union, largely neglected so far, namely the role of public finance, which we take to embrace not only taxation and public expenditure, but also the many regulatory, co-ordinating and non-budgetary activities in the economic field in existing economic unions.

Put another way, what we are talking about now is the transfer of resources from one part of the Community to another or, even more simply, help from the richer parts of the Community to the poorer.

Here it is necessary for the British in particular to tread with extreme caution. For Britain the first and absolute priority must be the restructuring of the Community budget so that less of it is devoted to agriculture and what remains is spent more efficiently.

At present the CAP is not even doing much to fulfil one of its original purposes of cushioning social change by helping people off the land and into industry. At the end of 1980, for instance, Signor Antonio Giolitti, the Community Commissioner for regional policy, reported in some detail that the CAP is actually encouraging rich farming regions to get richer rather than succouring the poorer areas. One of the reasons is that the Community's price support system is biased towards the products of northern Europe: milk, beet sugar, cereals and milk. Thus, in regional terms, the principal beneficiaries are the Paris basin, central and south-east England and northern Germany. Among the losers are much of Italy and southern France. Again, whereas in the mid-1960s about one third of Community farm spending went into structural improvements, by the end of the 1970s the proportion had been reduced to 5 per cent because of the constant pressure of the price support systems on the agricultural budget. In 1978 nearly half of CAP spending went on diary products alone.

The most striking figure of all is the amount which goes on the disposal of surpluses. According to a House of Commons written answer on 20 June 1980, such disposal accounted for 61 per cent of CAP spending in 1975, and 48 per cent of the Community budget as a whole. By 1979 the figures had advanced to 80 and 60 per cent respectively. That last figure is worth repeating: by 1979, 60 per cent of all Community spending was accounted for by the disposal of agricultural surpluses. There is plenty of scope for reform there before Britain starts advocating more grandiose plans for increasing Community expenditure. In any case the restructuring of the budget away from agriculture would itself release additional resources for spending in other fields, such as the regional and social policies.

It should never be forgotten either that any British government that even hinted at raising Community spending before the CAP was reformed would be in great danger of undermining its bargaining position − not to speak of a political furore at home. It has taken eight years of membership and attempted renegotiation to get where we are, with the promise of the restructuring of the budget accepted by the entire Community. The guarantee is that if the reform is not achieved within the next year or so, the Community's own resources will run out, thus compelling action to be taken. There can be therefore no question of talking too loudly about increasing Community activities, in so far as they involve higher spending, in the short to medium term.

Two other considerations ought to be borne in mind. First, Britain is not the only member of the Community which is at present concerned with cutting, or at least controlling, public expenditure in general. Suggestions that Community spending should go up while restraints are being applied at home are likely to fall on no more fertile ground in Paris and Bonn than in London. Second, it is important that the idea of increased expenditure in the longer term should not be seen as British special pleading: that is, another variant of the complaint that the Community must do more for Britain or risk the threat of withdrawal.

Once those reservations have been made, however, it still seems to me that the possibility of a greater role for public finance is worth reconsidering. Much of the basic data is provided in the MacDougall Report and has not gone significantly out of date. What the figures really show is how little the Community spends in its own right, and certainly as measured against spending by national governments.

Some of the essential findings of the Report can be summarised as follows:

(1) Public expenditure by members of the Community in 1975 was about 45 per cent of the gross product of the area as a whole (that is the weighted average for the individual states).

(2) Expenditure by all Community institutions is 0.7 per cent of gross product.

(3) The redistributive power of the Community's finances between member states is only about 1 per cent. That is partly because the Community budget is relatively so small and partly because neither the expenditures nor the revenues of the Community have a particularly strong redistributive effect in terms of the regions.

That is the starting point. The MacDougall Commission then went on to study how redistribution worked elsewhere, both in federations and in unitary states. The countries covered included Australia, Canada, the US, Switzerland, West Germany, France, Italy and the UK. Not the least interesting finding here was that the country with the most equal inter-regional income distribution was Australia, followed successively by Germany, the UK and Switzerland. After that France, the US and Canada were all grouped in a similar position. The country with the most unequal distribution was Italy. Furthermore, redistribution tends to take place as a deliberate political act whether a country is a unitary state like Britain or a federation like Switzerland. In Britain, for instance, the Rate Support Grant is part of a transfer of resources, as are various regional subsidies. The obligation to redistribute income, in short, appears to be taken for granted.

Redistribution is, of course, already taking place at a national level within the Community's member states, but what is most striking is the gap between what is achieved by national governments and the 1 per cent redistribution achieved by Community spending. By contrast, the MacDougall Commission found that public expenditure and taxation policies in the countries studied reduced regional inequalities in *per capita* incomes by an average of 40 per cent — by more in Australia and France and by less in the US and Germany.

The obvious question that arises is: could not the Com-

munity do more? To which the equally obvious answer
ought to be: not necessarily for its own sake. There is,
after all, very little point in spending money just to show
that you are all members of the same Community, and if
some of the functions envisaged are already financed by
national governments. Yet more subtle questions also
occur. For example: are there not some functions that
might be carried out more efficiently by the Community
as a whole? In that case, it would be not so much a matter
of new expenditure as a transfer of responsibilities from
national exchequers to Community institutions.

The MacDougall Report put forward several possibilities, the most significant of which are two related general
concepts rather than specific proposals. The first concept
is what the Report calls 'pre-federal integration'. This is
defined as completing the Common Market by the elimination of non-tariff barriers and other distortions to trade
and facilitating the freer movement of capital and labour.
There would be also increased cooperation in economic
and monetary policy, though falling short of monetary
union. It is assumed that the Community's political struc-
tures will go on developing both through political cooperation in the foreign policy field and through the direct
elections to the European Parliament which have since
taken place. The new element proposed is that public
expenditure at the Community level should rise to around
2–2.5 per cent of gross product, as against the present 0.7
per cent. We shall come back to the way these new Community funds might be raised and spent.

The second general concept put forward by MacDougall
is that of an emerging tier of Community government, or
at least 'a higher level of government than the member
state'. The theory behind it is that there might be policy
areas or particular issues where this new tier of government might be the most appropriate forum in which to
take decisions.

In this respect the Report has been already vindicated by events. The higher level of government has to some extent come into being through the development of the European Council. These thrice-yearly meetings of Community heads of state or government are at least theoretically capable of setting the general directions for the future of the Community. It might be argued that they ought to do more and perhaps need some backup machinery: for example it is sometimes not very clear to the officials who have to carry out the decisions what the heads of government, meeting alone, have decided. But there are some decisions which only the heads of government can take. The very existence of the European Council is evidence of the perceived need for a body that can go above the heads of the traditional institutions. It is also evidence of the way that the Community, in its decision-making processes, has been able to adapt to changing circumstances.

Indeed the European Council might be the best possible starting point for a new look at the Community's priorities in the rest of the 1980s. On the assumption that present disputes are going to be resolved, it might like to initiate studies of where the Community goes next. The British government might even take the lead in proposing that such studies should be set in train. Certainly there are many questions to be asked, perhaps the most important of which is: are there more activities which could be conducted more effectively by the Community as a whole than by national governments? A subsidiary question, which will become more pointed with the entry of Spain and Portugal, is whether a Community that does not actively attempt to reduce major disparities in income between member states can really be considered a Community. Some partial answers may be found in the work already done by the MacDougall Commission.

One of the main criteria set by MacDougall was the need

for 'economies of scale' — a term much more in vogue in the 1970s than it is today, but surely not yet invalidated. It does not apply only to the industrial field. Efforts to achieve a common foreign policy are themselves part of an attempt to bring about economies of scale in that they recognise that the members might be able to accomplish more collectively than as individuals, especially if they have broadly the same aims. A practical example, which might both save money and achieve greater results, would be a pooling of the development aid resources of the member states. Added together, these are considerable. The Community has already acted in this way through the Lomé Agreements with the African, Caribbean and Pacific countries. Not the least advantage — to both donor and recipient — is that such agreements can take the place of dozens of bilateral arrangements. Both sides also increase their bargaining power because they are negotiating in a wider forum. It is at least worth noting that even among the British critics of the Community, few attack the principle of Community aid, though they might have reservations about the details.

Still, under the broad head of economies of scale it is the industrial field that rightly commands most attention. The MacDougall Report singled out several sectors, under the main headings of civil nuclear engineering, defence research and development, civil aeronautics, space, telecommunications, computer science and automation, new sources of energy and medical research.

Nothing here has improved very much with time. Indeed in some respects the prospects of European cooperation have actually receded. The aerospace merger between the Dutch Fokker company and the West German Vereinigte Flugtechnische Werke (VFW) in the early 1970s, which at the time seemed a portent of the future, has since been unwound. So too has the altogether more ambitious pooling of computer resources between the Dutch Philips, the

French C-II and the West German Siemens companies. The private sector, even with some state prodding, has not found it easy to manage cross-frontier mergers.

The basic problems remain. What all the sectors listed by MacDougall have in common is that they are to some extent dependent on public funds and public purchasing, and require large-scale expenditure on research and development. They are in the main politically and strategically sensitive, in that certainly none of the major European countries would like to be deprived of them altogether, and therefore obliged to rely on outside suppliers. They are also in competition with highly developed companies in the US and, increasingly, Japan. There is no particular evidence nowadays that the Europeans are short on know-how, but they may be competing unnecessarily with each other, duplicating the costs of research and development and failing to reach their joint potential.

What has happened so far has been a series of *ad hoc* arrangements, sometimes bilateral, sometimes multilateral. It is true that there appears to have been one conspicuous success in the development of the European Airbus, but for the rest the *ad hoc* approach has had indifferent results. The British and the French, for instance, cooperated on the production of the Jaguar strike aircraft, but not on its selling. The French in fact found that it was in competition with their own national products. The British, Germans and Italians worked together on the Tornado multi-role combat aircraft, but hopelessly underestimated the costs and the difficulties to the point where it has been seriously questioned whether multilateral projects are more cost-effective than going it alone.

There has been a similar proliferation of ventures in the energy field. The British, the Dutch and the Germans participate in the Urenco project for uranium enrichment, but France belongs to a quite separate group known as Eurodif, which includes members from outside the European Community.

Of course, some of the issues here are highly sensitive. Defence collaboration is complicated by the fact that France does not belong to the military organisation of the Atlantic alliance. The French may have a different defence strategy and therefore different weapons requirements. Defence contracts also mean jobs, which means in turn that no country is eager to give up its own defence industries simply for the sake of international cooperation or even a more effective overall defence contribution. On the energy side, it is not surprising that efforts at collaboration are so diffuse, since the Community has no common energy policy, a subject that will be discussed in the next chapter.

And yet, theoretically, the arguments about economies of scale remain attractive. Europe is not doing as well as it might out of its series of *ad hoc* technology agreements. The European rival to IBM in the computer field has not emerged, either through Community cooperation or through national developments. In general, one senses that there has been a loss of direction. Everyone agrees that Europe ought to be able to do better, but nobody gives a lead.

Sir Harold Wilson, the former British Prime Minister, used to propose — before Britain became a member — that technology should be the Community's new dimension. Admittedly, he had a special interest. In those days it was widely believed, especially by the British, that we were superior in these matters. Playing the high technology card was one way of seeking to gain entry. Yet the idea of a technological Community is worth reconsidering now. Once again the initiative, to have any force, could best come from the European Council. If the Council were to seek an agenda of priorities for the 1980s, one item would have to be the question of what has happened to technological cooperation so far. Why has it been so diverse? Why has there been so little Community direction? Could there not be areas of research and development which the Community could fund, if necessary with new resources?

The possibility of political complications should not be overlooked. It is already apparent in the Community's approach to the old industries, such as steel and shipbuilding. Some countries – West Germany is the outstanding example – tend to regard Community efforts to limit output as unduly interventionist and restrictive of competition. Mrs Thatcher's government leans the same way, though its successor could have different priorities. This conflict of philosophies between governments which believe in interventionism and those which prefer to rely on market forces is always likely to exist, and could become greater if the Community had stronger powers over industrial policy.

Nevertheless, the fact remains that the EEC's industrial cooperation lags behind what has been achieved in foreign policy. The real issue at stake is how far it wants to be a Community, whether it really welcomes the process of sharing what are, after all, common problems, even if the burden is unequal. Each member state, with the possible exceptions of Greece and Ireland, has the problems of old and declining industries and the need to find new ones at the national level. The challenge is twofold: how to help those areas and those people suffering from industrial decline, and how best to direct investment and industrial cooperation in the future.

In the old days, in the Community of the Six and before the energy crisis, there would have been no doubt. There would have been a summit communiqué calling for a blueprint for action, even if the action was not always taken. Since then Europe has tended to lose faith in its own dynamism. If the Community does not seek such a blueprint now, it will be running away from its own problems, and in danger of becoming a Community only in name. Not everything, perhaps very little, can be done at the

Community level. But at least the whole question of industrial policy and the social effects of industrial change should be placed at the head of the EEC agenda. If it leads to a call for a greater transfer of resources between one member state and another, why not? That is what belonging to a Community is supposed to be about. It would be a very strange Community that ducked the issue altogether, merely in response to a time of financial stringency. There might even be savings from economies of scale.

Yet there is another reason for looking again at the need for higher Community spending and greater resource transfers. It concerns enlargement. The argument is partly moral, though also political.

In the original Community, disparities of income did not seem to matter very much. There was the major exception of southern Italy, but the Community was meant to cope with it, and might have done so rather better if the Italians themselves had been more demanding. The first enlargement did not make all that much difference. Denmark was already rich. Britain, for all its economic problems, could not reasonably claim to be all that poor. Ireland was small enough to be helped in a major way even under existing Community policies. It is rare to come across anyone who begrudges what the common agricultural policy has done for the Irish economy or what membership of the Community has done for Irish self-confidence, except perhaps in Ulster. Greece, too, might be assimilated without any great changes in Community policies.

But with the potential accession of Spain and Portugal we enter a different world. We do so even more so if Turkey is included on the admittedly more distant horizon. Here are countries with severe regional problems of their own, and with a level of development way below that of mainstream Europe. In the years of high economic growth – up to 1973 – there was a kind of *de facto* interdependence between the prospective new members and the existing Common Market. Greece, Spain, Portugal and Turkey were a source of labour which contributed to the Community's economic expansion. In return, they benefited from their migrant workers sending part of their earnings back home, and perhaps eventually from the repatriation of some skills.

The period up to 1973 was also one of high outside investment in what one might call, without being pejorative, peripheral Europe. Turkey had one of the highest growth rates in the Western world — an average of 8 per cent a year in real terms. As for Spain, people were talking of the latest European economic miracle, after Germany, Italy and Austria.

The position today is transformed. Because of slower growth, the Community has less need for migrant workers, except perhaps in the most menial occupations. Besides, West Germany in particular believes that it has already run up against severe social problems by admitting so many non-German-speaking workers whose children, like those of Commonwealth and Pakistani immigrants in Britain, have to go to local schools. (One section of West Berlin is now known as the third biggest Turkish city in the world, after Istanbul and Ankara.) The flow of migrants' remittances to the home countries has much diminished. So has the level of investment.

Interdependence between the Community and the applicants has thus given way to a kind of dependence on the part of the applicants. They used to have high growth: they probably still have high expectations, which they look to the Community to fulfil. At the same time, they remain relatively backward in economic terms. Agriculture is still predominant in their economies, but it is not always especially productive. In so far as there has been a movement away from the land, it may only have increased urban unemployment. The infrastructure of Spain, Portugal and Turkey hardly bears comparison with mainstream Europe.

These generalised remarks can be put in statistical form. The figures, taken from the *Bulletin of the European Communities,* Supplement 3/78, may be slightly out of date, but they appear to be the best that the European Commission has to offer in its considerations of the further enlargement of the Community. *Per capita* income in Portugal is only one third of the Community average. In Spain it is 54 per cent and in Greece 44 per cent. A Turkish figure has not yet been given in this context because Turkish membership is rather further away, but it would be the poorest of the lot.

It is plain that we are dealing here with incomes disparities of a kind not previously experienced by the Community. Ireland, the poorest member of the Community of the Nine, had a *per capita* income that was 47 per cent of the Community average, but Ireland has a population of less than 3.5 million. The population of Greece is 9.5 million, that of Portugal around 10 million, and the Spanish population is nearly 38 million. The population of Turkey is over 45 million.

And yet Spain and Portugal and eventually Turkey are the countries that want to join. It is a tribute to the success of the Community so far that they should wish to do so. After all, there has been no comparable rush to join Comecon, the trading group of the Soviet Union and the East European states. (Some of those might like to join the Community too, if they had the chance.) But it might be reasonably asked whether Europe has something more to offer in the way of the transfer of resources than is at present on the agenda.

There is, first of all, a matter of pride. If you go from (say) Manchester to Hamburg today, you might note that the Germans are much richer and in some ways perhaps more efficient. But the similarities would still outweight the differences. Both are modern urban societies. The people in the two cities are probably discussing much the same questions: what has happened, for instance, to educational standards? What are the effects of recession and the decline of old industries, and what is to be done about the inner-city areas, given the drift of the more affluent part of the population towards the suburbs? How do you finance the sort of social services that people have come to expect? In other words, you would be living in recognisably the same world.

It is quite different if you go to Lisbon. The poverty is visible. A taxi trip across half the city can cost so little that you can offend the driver by trying to compensate through overtipping. The attitudes are different, too. The state has never reached that level of expenditure on social policy which tends to be taken for granted in much of Western Europe. Nor has the infrastructure been developed. People seem to live with inequalities in a way that is hard to imagine in Britain, France, West Germany or Scandinavia. Portugal is economically and − some would say − socially backward compared to the great bulk of the existing Community.

The question arises of what sort of Community it would be that did little or nothing directly to raise the living standards of its poorest members. It can be put in both practical and moral terms. Practically, the new members will need some stake in the Community that goes beyond participating in discussions on foreign policy. Their populations will need some tangible benefits, especially since the first effects of the reduction of tariff barriers could be economically and socially painful. It is hard to see that it would be a politically healthy development if the new members were to start to behave like Britain and claim that the advantages of belonging to the Community were not all that had been promised. There are some signs that Greece is already beginning to make this claim. Mr Andreas Papandreou, the Greek Socialist leader, sounds remarkably like some British politicians in his reluctance to come to terms with membership and his call for a referendum on whether Greece stays in. The Community ought at least to have a response that it is ready to do something to raise the Greek level of economic development.

Morally, it seems to me intolerable that poor new members should be allowed to join what is in many ways a rich man's club without the club then trying to reduce disparities in income. That is what is meant by the matter of pride. Spain and Portugal want to come in: they ought to have some incentive to stay. The best approach would be a deliberate effort to raise their living standards and to improve their infrastructure by some transfer of resources.

There is enormous room for argument about how that could be done. There could be an expansion of the existing regional and social policies. More ambitiously, there could be some kind of budget equalisation scheme under which the Community agreed to make a straight financial transfer to its poorer members. The MacDougall Report suggested the possibility of some limited, but unconditional, redistribution along the following lines:

> The Community might establish a fiscal equalisation mechanisms, but setting an unusually low minimum standard of, say, 65 per cent of the Community average fiscal capacity. . . .
>
> Such a system might be intended to assure to poor, small and peripheral member states economic, welfare and public service standards not too far below those of the main body of the Community. For prospective member states it could serve to provide some general financial underpinning for the economic risks of joining the customs union.

There is another argument for an effort to raise the level of development in the poorer member states, and it would certainly have been put in the past. It is that Community investment in improving the infrastructure of (say)

Spain and Portugal would benefit the Community as a whole. It would do so because it would raise the level of economic activity throughout the Community, in that many of the contracts would go to companies in the industrialised member states. There would therefore be a mutually beneficial effect. The old members would have provided the technology and received some of the business, while the new members would have absorbed the investment and provided some of the labour, thereby lessening unemployment and raising the local standard of living.

Today such arguments are out of fashion, along with Keynesian economics and counter-cyclical economic policy. Indeed one sometimes wonders if politicians of today would ever have permitted Marshall Aid, if they had been in power at the time. But fashions can change very quickly. The idea of major Community investment in Spain and Portugal is at least worth keeping in reserve.

The possible variations on resource transfer are almost infinite. Until the Community's present problems of restructuring the budget are resolved, it is not an immediate issue, but with further enlargement it will come. Moreover, as I have tried to outline, there may be a case for increasing spending even in the existing Community in such areas as research and development, advanced technology and alleviating the effects of industrial and social change.

The common thread is that if the Community is to be dynamic, at some stage either the 1 per cent VAT ceiling on the Community's own resources will have to be lifted, or new sources of revenue found. That stage is not yet, but the question has to be faced. Unless we want to stop the Community in its tracks, it will need more financial resources. That is what Britain ought to be thinking about beyond the reform of the CAP. How should the resources be raised, and for which purposes? Without any special pleading we now have the opportunity to make a contribution to thinking on this subject.

The conventional view, shared by MacDougall, that the simplest way to increase revenues would be to seek more from VAT, has a lot to be said for it. However, an alternative of at least additional source might be found from energy, as we shall see in the next chapter.

CHAPTER 6

The Energy Card

Energy ought to be easy. It is the one area where Britain has something in abundance which the rest of the Community has not. It is not only North Sea oil and gas, though those are the most obvious attractions. There is also coal and the modern technologies that go with it, such as gasification. Not least, Britain has long experience of nuclear power. There must be something seriously wrong with any government which fails to draw foreign policy conclusions from such a surfeit of resources in a world where future energy supplies have become a matter of major concern.

It is worth considering first what Britain in 1981 would have been like if there had been no North Sea oil and gas. It would have been very different from the country we know today. Almost certainly, there would have been a permanent balance of payments crisis – much greater than the periodic crises of the 1960s and 1970s – because we would have continued to be dependent on imported oil at a time when oil prices were generally rising sharply. In fact, we have become a net oil exporter and British balance of payments crises have become a thing of the past. One rather melancholy chapter in British economic history has been closed for some time to come.

If we had continued to be dependent on oil imports,

certain other consequences would have followed. It is quite likely that we should have been down to a one-dollar pound, as seemed the trend only a few years ago. There would then have been enormous pressures – unlikely to be fully resisted – for the imposition of import controls. One leaves it to economists to judge how far this would have added to inflation, but the point is that we should have been living in a quite different political and economic environment.

More than just the balance of payments is involved. North Sea oil and gas have contributed directly to government revenues – to the tune of £4–5 billion in 1980–81 and perhaps twice as much or more in two or three years' time. Already in 1981 government revenues from the North Sea are the equivalent of about eight pence in the pound on the standard rate of income tax. If those revenues were not there, they would have to be found from somewhere else. Alternatively, we should simply have had a much lower standard of living.

There is another fact about energy which needs to be taken into account. The steep jump in oil prices in late 1973 was the biggest single shock ever administered to the postwar economic and political system. In 1948 the posted price of Saudi Arabian crude was $2.06 a barrel. Throughout most of the 1950s and 1960s it was less than $2. In 1974, after the latest Middle East war in which the Arabs for the first time used the 'oil weapon', it rose to $11.65. There have been times since when the price of a barrel of oil has been remarkably similar to the old official price per ounce of gold – $35, and sometimes higher.

There is room for all sorts of arguments here. Why did the oil producers keep the price so low for so long? Why did the consumers allow them to do so? (That question is more subtle, but still relevant.) Why did people not start talking earlier about the finite nature of existing resources? How far is it all to do with politics? If there had been no

Palestinian problem in the Middle East, would we have gone on much as before, with an oil price steadily falling in real terms and no questions raised about security of supplies? And if so, for how long?

The answers to those questions, even if they could be established, lie beyond the scope of this book. What the oil crisis of 1973–74 did, however, was to draw attention to the arbitrary nature of the oil price, the uncertainty about supplies — which even in the best of circumstances will not go on for ever — and the overdependence of the industrialised countries on imported energy, much of it from the Middle East. A large part of international politics ever since has been about how to adjust to this situation.

Britain is lucky, but is not immune. Clearly she could survive a disruption of international energy supplies more easily than most countries because of her indigenous resources. But, equally clearly, she would suffer from a major disruption because Britain cannot shut herself off from the rest of the world. The chief foreign policy question is therefore whether Britain's energy resources can be put to any other use apart from domestic self-sufficiency. Is there not an external dimension?

It is necessary to have a sense of perspective here. Britain's oil reserves are large in relation to her own requirements over the next 15–20 years, but they are tiny when measured against world reserves. The country has already achieved net self-sufficiency, but British oil output is less than 3 per cent of the world total. The figures will change no doubt with new discoveries, though not necessarily in the British favour. At present, British North Sea oil reserves account for only 2.4 per cent of proven world reserves.

Yet there are other ways of looking at it. In *North Sea Oil and Gas and British Foreign Policy* (Royal Institute of International Affairs, 1980), Ray Dafter and Ian Davidson have sought to put the figures in a European context. Current net British self-sufficiency is equivalent to about 1.8 million barrels of oil a day, and has been attained. Yet British output could rise in the next year or two to 2.5 million barrels daily or even 3 million, and could remain there for a good decade or so. That leaves a substantial surplus. Let us be modest about it and say that the surplus is only 0.7 million barrels daily. Even then, it is still the equivalent of 25 per cent of net West German oil imports or 7 per cent of the total oil imports of the European Community.

Those figures are not trivial. Indeed it is quite striking that the International Energy Agency (IEA), the body set up after the 1973–74 crisis to monitor oil supplies and to provide mutual help in the case of emergencies, regards a shortfall of 7 per cent in the oil supplies of any one of its members, or of the group as a whole, as a *prima facie* case for putting its support operations into motion. Theoretically at least, Britain alone has the capacity to do that for the entire European Community. It would not do much to relieve a major crisis such as the collapse of output in Saudi Arabia, but it could do a great deal to relieve a minor one: for instance, if the Iran–Iraqi war of 1980–81 had had more serious consequences for oil production that it did.

The Dafter–Davidson thesis is that the British surplus should be kept in reservoirs in the North Sea for use by the rest of the Community if an emergency arises. In making such an offer, Britain should seek to secure other Common Market reforms, notably of the common agricultural policy. As the authors put it:

> If the UK were to announce that it intended to secure as rapid a development of the North Sea as possible; that it intended to hold down production to a level close to net self-sufficiency in normal times of supply and demand; and that it would open the taps in times

of shortage for the benefit of customers in the European Community, then this would represent the maximum that the UK could offer, and a great deal more than is being offered by any other oil-producing country.

They also note:

> We know that the other Community countries are anxious for Britain to make such an offer. At a meeting of the Council of Energy Ministers in December 1979, shortly after the Dublin Summit, France and Germany explicitly proposed that there should be an agreement on the expansion of Community hydrocarbon production in the event of a sub-crisis, and they were supported by five other member states. The proposal was rejected by Britain and Holland.

(Holland, like Britain, is a major gas producer.)

The principal practical objection to the Dafter–Davidson idea is said in official British circles to be one of cost. The storage of the oil in the reservoirs would have to be paid for, and none of the Community members has come rushing forward with offers of financial support. Yet it is an attractive proposal worth further consideration. It does not seem to me, however, to be adequate in itself. It smacks, as the authors admit, of the lowest common denominator.

The thesis also suffers from an excess of the authors' own rationalism. It assumes that because they have worked out that this is the most that Britain can reasonably offer, the offer will therefore be accepted. It makes no allowance for the haggles – for the playing for big stakes – which have to be regarded as a natural part of Community life, just as they are of national politics. The playing of the energy card could be an altogether more ambitious enterprise.

The fact is that despite Britain's relative advantages, energy is a common problem. Arguably it is the biggest single problem facing the majority of the member states, and is likely to continue so for the foreseeable future. No member of the Community can solve it alone. The days after the 1973—74 crisis when it was possible to go off to Iran or Saudi Arabia in search of a bilateral deal on oil supplies are over. Instability in those countries leads to trouble for the whole of Europe and, as we now know, those instabilities can occur. That is one reason why Europe has moved in search of a common foreign policy.

Yet there is also a case for going further. One of the main justifications of the Community's initiative in the Middle East is an attempt to keep the oil flowing by preventing political disruptions. In short, the energy crisis at least had the beneficial side-effect of persuading the EEC to act more closely in concert. It may be time now to go ahead and do something about energy directly.

The trouble about energy cooperation as it exists in the Community so far is that it is practically all *ad hoc*. It has no treaty basis. On a whole range of other issues — agriculture, regional policy, transport or competition — ministers may spend days, weeks or even years trying to reach agreement within a broadly accepted framework of rules. On energy policy there is no such compulsion and no agreed framework.

Yet if the Community were being founded today, energy policy, along with foreign policy cooperation, would almost certainly be one of the principal elements. It is open to Britain now — with all its assets of oil, gas, coal and nuclear experience — to take the initiative in proposing the formation of a European Energy Community, or at least of a common energy policy. Such a policy would not mean simply pooling existing energy resources, though that would be involved. It would also mean investing in energy for the future and dealing with the rest of the world on energy matters as a single entity. It would be in many ways the logical sequence to the pursuit of a common foreign policy.

If necessary, the common energy policy or Energy Community could be funded by a small levy – or common external tariff – on imported energy supplies from third countries, much on the lines of the CAP. Britain would be a clear beneficiary, but the Community could gain too from having a stronger assurance that its future energy requirements were being looked after. It is a case here – as it was in the founding of the Community – of the whole being considerably greater than the sum of the parts.

It will not have escaped notice either that if the Community needs a new 'own resource' when the present 1 per cent ceiling on the VAT contributions has been reached, one way forward might be the imported energy levy. Again it would benefit Britain, but at least there could be a satisfactory marriage between a continental Community whose interests appear to lie in supporting agriculture and an offshore island whose resources are different. It is the best balance that has been conceived so far. One way or another, one would expect a British government to pursue it.

There are only two other points to be made. The first is that the EEC is already benefiting from British oil, but that Britain is failing to seek any political advantage. The second is that if the British government does not believe that that there is an energy card to play, others do.

The pattern of European oil imports has already changed markedly since North Sea oil began to flow. In 1980, for example, Britain became West Germany's second largest oil supplier, and a fairly reliable one at that. At the same time, about 60 per cent of British oil exports were going to the European Community as a whole. It seems to me extraordinary that any British government should accept that purely as a random market development. Of course, Britain has to export the oil somewhere, and Europe, for obvious reasons, is a likely destination. What is so strange, however, is Britain should be in dispute with the Community about matters largely to do with agriculture, yet should be supplying member countries with increasing amounts of oil and failing to draw any connection between the two. Agriculture was in many ways yesterday's problem. Energy is today's and tomorrow's. The oil is already flowing to Europe, but Britain has so far failed to seek any compensating political reward. It is as if it were all happening by accident, with no foreign policy conclusions to be drawn.

The initiative lies with Britain. It is the only member with the resources credibly to propose a common energy policy. And the rest of the Community knows that this is so, because whenever Britain starts to talk about energy, the Community begins to listen. The energy card is the one that no other member holds, and it is sheer timidity, or maybe just a surfeit of defeatism, not to play it. Failure to use the card means wasting, not conserving it, because the oil is being consumed in any case.

Perhaps one should not expect too much. The Tory government which came to power in 1979 has been no more adept than its Labour predecessor of 1974–79 in deciding what to do with the oil revenues at home, except to spend them while allowing the pretence to continue that the bonanza is still to come. A government that cannot make up its mind about the domestic benefits of North Sea oil is unlikely to do very well in translating them into foreign policy.

Yet in the 1980s and 1990s energy is the best card we have. Think, as I wrote at the beginning of this chapter, what Britain would have been like now without North Sea oil. No one should say that we never had a chance. It might be exploited in Europe as well as at home.

CHAPTER 7

A Personal View

So, can we save the Common Market? It seems to me that the answer is yes, though the experience so far has been pretty dreary. For over 20 years — almost a generation — the Market has been a key issue in British politics. It has been one of the main factors in the divisions in the Labour Party from Hugh Gaitskell onwards. But there has not been a straight left–right split. The Tories, too, have their anti-Marketeers, apparently with considerable support in the constituencies. The European Reform Group, which was founded in 1980 under the auspices of the Conservative MP Mr Teddy Taylor, is basically as hostile to British membership as some of its Labour counterparts such as the Common Market Safeguards Committee. As the opinion polls show, the present state of affairs is clearly regarded as unsatisfactory by a large part of the British electorate.

It also has to be admitted that many of the critics are right. It is hard to disagree with Professor A. J. Brown of the University of Leeds when he argues that: 'Financially, the Communities constitute a club for agricultural price maintenance with minor philanthropic sideshows' (quoted in *Britain in Europe,* edited by William Wallace, Heinemann, 1980). There is a fundamental difference between a country such as Britain, with a small number of farmers and an interest in cheap food, and the bulk of the rest of the Community, which has large farming populations and which therefore wants to keep up farm prices. Again there are differences of history that cannot be eradicated overnight. The clichés are true. Britain is an offshore island. Its history has been rooted in non-involvement in Europe and reliance on the open seas. English nationalism began with the break with Rome under Henry VIII. That is what is taught in the schools as part of the country's heritage. France, by contrast, has always been a European power, even when it has been at odds with its neighbours.

It may be, of course, that we have made mistakes, the greatest of which was not to be in at the beginning when the rules were being formed. Yet the fact remains that after all these years, after one formal renegotiation and a subsequent referendum, Britain is at best a reluctant member.

If there were to be another referendum tomorrow, what would happen? Like practically everything put by the pollsters, that is a hypothetical question. There is not going to be another referendum tomorrow. What we have is a government which claims to be committed to Europe, which has the Brussels agreement on which to build, yet which has to face a general election in 1983 or 1984. That is not a great deal of time in which to convince the electorate of the benefits of membership and to take the issue out of British politics.

The choice for the government seems to lie between seeking to patch up something which would make belonging to the Community less of an irritant, though still perhaps a bad-tempered affair, and the bolder approach of trying to make membership both natural and desirable. As suggested in the previous chapter, energy would be the best card to play. It is the one area where Britain has something that the rest of the Community has not. It should be played for all that it is worth.

Yet the main thesis of this book is that the impetus for

a happier, more harmonious Community will have to come from the top. The European Council is now the Community's best hope. It is from there that new initiatives will have to come, which is why I have suggested that the British should call for the Council to set an agenda of priorities for the rest of the decade. From the British point of view, it is too late simply to hope that the Community will evolve in an acceptable way. Equally, British calls for reform cannot be left to the Foreign Office. They will have to be coordinated between all relevant departments and closely watched by the Prime Minister. There is no time left to afford any more mistakes.

It is for the same reason — that reform must come from the top — that some of the Community's institutions have scarcely been mentioned. They have been discussed endlessly before. The European Parliament, for example, seems to me to be a worthy enough body. It is regrettable, and not its fault, that direct elections were not introduced until 1979. It may serve a useful function in drawing people's attention to the fact that the Community does believe in parliamentary democracy and not simply rule by bureaucrats, but its time has not yet come. It is wholly irrelevant to the timetable of major reform of the Community within the next couple of years.

As for the Commission, it is a commonplace that it is supposed to be hopelessly demoralised, constantly and often unfairly criticised for seeking harmonisation for harmonisation's sake. It is probably also true that it carries a good deal of dead wood. Yet it is hard to see how it can reform itself.

Proposals for the reform of the EEC's institutions have been made many times, most recently at the instigation of the European Council itself, which had in turn been prompted to act by President Giscard d'Estaing. A 'Committee of Three Wise Men' was set up:

to consider the adjustments to the machinery and procedures of the institutions which are required for the proper operation of the Communities on the basis of and in compliance with the Treaties, including their institutional arrangements, and for progress towards European Union. It [the Council] emphasises the interest it attaches to having available specific proposals in this connection which may be implemented swiftly and which take into account experience to date and the prospective enlargement to 12. (*Report on European Institutions,* Commission of the European Communities, 1979.)

One of the members was Mr Edmund Dell, the former British Trade Secretary.

The Committee talked to everyone necessary, from heads of state or government downwards, and duly reported in October 1979. It made a number of sensible observations and some relatively modest suggestions. So far as I know none have yet been taken up.

For instance, the Committee noted that the Commission had 'lost much of its independent prestige'. Since enlargement, the increase in numbers of Commissioners:

made it impossible to give equally meaningful portfolios to them all; in practice this has led to an overload of work for some Commissioners, frustration for others. The Commission has no strong image as a team: it has been the actions of its President or individual members that have made most impression on the world outside. In its organisation generally, there is a lack of collegiate management and no collective policy approach. Inadequate overall planning, and lack of communication between Commissioners and other levels of the administration, have adversely affected both efficiency and morale among the Commission's staff.

Strong words, from which few would dissent. The Committee recommended, echoing the earlier Spierenburg Report on the workings of the Commission, that in future there should be only one Commissioner per member country. The switch to the new principle, it said, 'must be made at the next re-appointment of the Commission, which usefully coincides with Greek accession' (January 1981). It commented: 'If the will cannot be found to act at this stage, it will certainly not be found at any later date.'

January 1981 came and went. The proposal of one Commissioner per member country was not implemented. Instead there was a most unseemly scramble on the night that the portfolios were distributed. Mr Christopher Tugendhat, one of the two British Commissioners, had to ring up Mrs Thatcher to request her aid to prevent some of his powers being taken away from him. The Prime Minister's intervention was successful, but one of the results was that Mr Michael O'Kennedy, the new Irish Commissioner, was left with virtually no role. There was also a certain amount of bad blood.

The report of the three wise men is again worth consulting on the matter of COREPER, the Committee of Permanent Representatives, of ambassadors, to the Community of the member states. It is sometimes said that COREPER ought to be more efficient, and should have more responsibilities, including the power to take decisions without having to wait for the Council of Ministers. Yet, as the report remarks: 'The most important factor in allowing COREPER to function well is, in fact, efficient coordination of Community business at home.' Indeed it would be highly irresponsible and politically dangerous to allow ambassadors to take decisions if they do not know what domestic policy is, or if policy at home has not yet been worked out.

Here again, the lead has to come from the top. Neither

the Commission nor COREPER can do very much to reform themselves. Yet if the European Council can ask for
recommendations on reforming the institutions, if the
recommendations produced are perfectly sensible, and if
the Council then ignores them, the prospects for reform
are dim. Equally, if member states do not know what they
want from the Community and cannot give proper, coordinated instructions to their permanent representatives
in Brussels, it is not surprising that Community procedures
sometimes look less than streamlined.

These questions are more urgent for the British than for
any other member. It is they, after all, who need reform if
the electorate is to be convinced of the benefits of staying
in. The rest of the Community might be content to adopt
the old British practice of simply muddling through. Oddly
enough, Europe seems to be one of the few areas where
Britain is reluctant to allow that doctrine to apply. British
opinion is impatient with the Community, but no British
government has yet worked out an agenda of its requirements.

The political case for membership is stronger than it has
ever been. It would be very cold outside. In the 1950s the
reason why few Britons seriously entertained the idea of
going in at the start was that Britain was not accustomed
to think in that way. It was the Anglo–American relationship and then the Commonwealth that mattered. It was
good for Europe to get together, but that meant continental Europe, of which Britain was not part.

Since then Europe has grown stronger and the US relatively weaker. The Commonwealth has gone its own
diverse ways, unlikely to be led by Britain and with little
to offer in the way of trade, let alone security. True, the
EEC is not a defence community. Any suggestion that it
should be has been carefully avoided in this book. For
defence we have NATO and we need the Atlantic alliance.
But it is a community of interests: in trade, in foreign

policy and even in cultural traditions. It is also democratic. Greece and Portugal were members of NATO while living under dictatorships; it is almost inconceivable that any totalitarian state − left or right − could be accepted in the European Community. In a world of blocs it is the most natural bloc to turn to. It is the best way of talking to other blocs, including the US. For all those reasons, I think that if there were another referendum Britain would still vote to stay in. There remain enough leading British politicians to argue the case, which is, at its crudest, that there is nowhere else to go.

There is another factor. It used to be said, and indeed is sometimes said today, that the purpose of the Community is to prevent another Franco−German war. At the time of the founding of the Coal and Steel Community in the early 1950s that was probably the case, in that it locked the war-making industries together. Those were the days of low technology. The purpose has been long since achieved. It is inconceivable to me that two neighbouring advanced industrial democracies could go to war with each other. Modern technology means that they could destroy each other overnight. Anyone who suggests the need to keep the French and Germans together as a justification for the Community in the 1980s is living in the past.

Yet there is another kind of conflict that Europe might prevent, or at least diminish. To many in Britain the Community might seem a troublesome place. Not only are there pseudo-wars about fish, lamb and apples, but there are also potential civil wars: in Spain, in the two parts of Ireland, perhaps in the linguistic conflicts in Belgium. What is notable is that while the Basques may have quarrels with the Spanish authorities, and their own cultural and nationalist reasons for doing so, they do not appear to have quarrels with Europe.

Ireland is the most conspicuous example. Relations between Dublin and London may not yet be ideal, but at least they have become closer and more understanding since the countries belonged to the same Community. It is the same with relations between the Republic of Ireland and Ulster. No one would pretend that the troubles are anything like over, but the places where Catholic and Protestant politicians talk to each other are Brussels and Strasbourg, and the subjects that they talk about are the common agricultural policy and the workings of the regional and social funds. It is the most that has been done so far to resolve the Irish question. Europe should not be underestimated as a unifying factor. Regional conflicts may survive, but at least there is acceptance of living under a common umbrella. That is an advance not to be lightly thrown away. The Community has made civil war in Europe less likely.

For years ahead, the European Community is probably not going to be the body that the founding fathers or their most devoted followers envisaged, or that even I, as a modest European, would have hoped for. I should have liked to see the abolition of passports for travel between one member state and another, or automatic common Community citizenship, a far greater interchange between British and European universities, even an exchange of personnel between British and fellow members' government departments, an end to the sillier manifestations of British and French prejudices.

Like many others, I underestimated the problems. I forgot about the British tendency to need a scapegoat for their ills. I assumed that British nationalism with a large 'N' was a thing of the past, to be absorbed in a wider community, and that Anglo–French rivalries would be submerged under a common purpose. European nationalism with a small 'n' seemed, and seems, a more attractive attribute. The fault is not only on the British side, especially in Anglo–French relations. If the British and the French could reach a greater mutual understanding, Europe could be transformed as well – and not to the detriment of West Germany or the smaller members. I overestimated the readiness of Europe to come to terms with a belated, in some way recidivist, but still desirable recruit. Most of us, we should admit, have been wrong about Europe at some time or other.

Some of the more emotive language about Europe have scarcely been touched on: sovereignty, integration, the prospect of a United States of Europe. The argument about sovereignty seems to me irrelevant, in that it is not self-evident that we make good use of what sovereignty we have. Some sovereignty has already been surrendered to NATO and to the International Monetary Fund without any feeling of national loss and for some benefit. In any case, it is a matter of pooling rather than surrender: we do have some bargaining power.

As for integration, it was referred to in the phrase of the MacDougall Report as 'pre-federal'. The point about that is that some of the proposals in the Report could, and should, be adopted for their own sake without any binding commitment to going down the federalist road. Again, we accept constraints from the IMF without anyone arguing that everyone has to have the same currency. We do it because we think that it is in our own best interests. A United States of Europe is not seriously on the agenda for the foreseeable future. What we are talking about is agreeing on a formula for greater European cooperation that goes beyond a customs union and which should establish a European identity.

The day before I completed this book, I went to talk to a conference of British officials at the Civil Service College in Sunningdale on the subject of Britain and Europe. It was a depressing experience. Some of them had been involved in the original abortive negotiations on British entry. Most of them had been asked from time to time to come up with ways of making membership more bene-

ficial – for instance, by securing more Community funds
for the Department of the Environment. There was an
overwhelming sense of failure. In the course of an internal
argument around the table about why the common fisheries
policy had not been included in the Wilson–Callaghan
renegotiation, the people from the Ministry of Agriculture
tended to blame the Foreign Office, and vice versa.
Between them they decided to blame the politicians.

Even more striking was the cynicism about the Brussels
agreement. Why, the civil servants asked, should we believe
that the Community would honour it? Britain had never
achieved reform in Europe before, so why should it do so
now? Besides, none of them showed the slightest idea of
the sort of reforms they wanted, except to agree that
membership was probably desirable for reasons of foreign
policy, a subject which several of them said they knew
little about.

Most depressing of all was the apparent belief among the
home civil servants that membership of the Community
was a necessary penance imposed by the Foreign Office
without compensating benefits. Lest it appear that I
generalise too much on the basis of one meeting, I should
add that it was simply a summation of the attitudes of the
domestic civil service over the years. One went away convinced that if Britain were to leave the Community, some
other external adventure would have to be invented in
order to save the British from themselves. The fact is that
the Community is a useful scapegoat for ills which are our
own; it could be also the best remedy, if we wanted a cure.
In continuing to debate the merits or demerits of membership, without being able to put forward our own proposals
for change, we are debating, even wallowing in, our own
decline.

Of course there are special problems for Britain, as the
experience of the last two or three decades has shown. But
the government has the opportunity to get it right this

time. The ideal result would be one where the British people chose to belong to Europe not because there was nowhere else to go, but because that was where they began to feel at home. Failure would be that British membership should continue as a major issue in British politics. In the latter case, the choice would lie between holding together an increasingly unhappy marriage, and divorce. It is hard to see how either would benefit either Europe or Britain.

The final answer to the question 'Can we save the Common Market?' is 'Yes, provided that the British and continental governments realise what is at stake and make the efforts from the top.' The awful reservation is that if Britain and Europe had realised that before, none of us would be in our present position.

INDEX

113